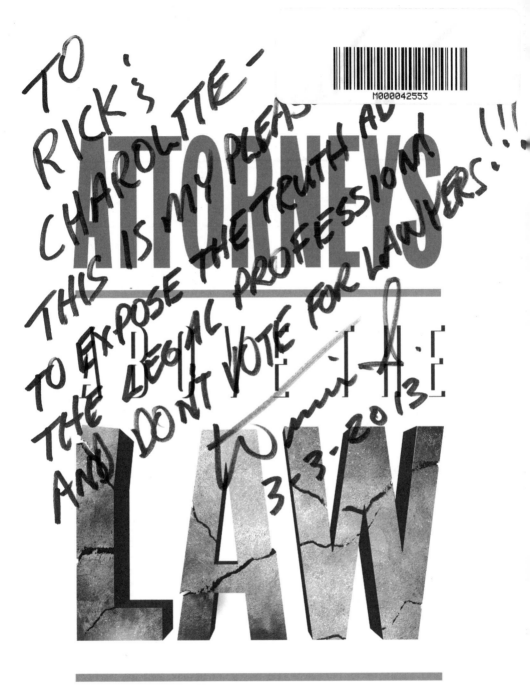

ATTORNEYS

AT THE

LAW

DENNIS SCHUELKE

TO RICK'S CHAROLTTE -
THIS IS MY PLEASE
TO EXPOSE THE TRUTH ABOUT
THE LEGAL PROFESSION!
AND DON'T VOTE FOR LAWYERS!!!

Dennis Schuelke
3-3-2013

Catchum Lion Enterprises, LLC.

© 2011 Catchum Lion Enterprises, LLC.

Library of Congress Control Number: 2011917006

Book Design: Birdsong Creative, Inc.
Franklin, TN | www.birdsongcreative.com

Edited by Alice Sullivan, www.alicesullivan.com

ISBN 9780983946809

www.AttorneysAboveTheLaw.com

TABLE OF CONTENTS

Preface. 1

INTRODUCTION 9

CHAPTER 1: Bamboozled and Chapped 13

CHAPTER 2: It Would Have Been Nice 27

CHAPTER 3: The Root of It All. 61

CHAPTER 4: Hide and Go Seek With Evidence 69

CHAPTER 5: Arbitration Trial 81

CHAPTER 6: The Verdict 119

CHAPTER 7: Arbitration Reconsideration 129

CHAPTER 8: Trickum Back. 157

CHAPTER 9: My Confession. 165

CHAPTER 10: Conclusion. 177

Recommendations 183

Acknowledgments 193

DEDICATION

THIS BOOK IS DEDICATED TO MY FATHER who was born in Nebraska and raised during the great depression. During the 1950s, he moved to Iowa as a farmer and also became an agricultural land improvement contractor. He died April 14, 2009. He suffered through a nearly fatal body burn, multiple strokes, and a heart attack; still, he always hoped justice would be served against my attorney, as my father was well aware of our losses and the job the attorney did for himself.

Well, Father, I'm sorry your wishes didn't come to fruition while you were with us here on earth, but it wasn't because I didn't try. You were a man of unimaginable drive, pride, accomplishments, honor, and integrity, and I can only hope your wishes are granted to view from above as this message travels across the land to alert hardworking Americans about attorneys like this one in particular.

Not all people have your integrity, Dad, and I've learned it the hard way. That's OK because there isn't anything worth gaining in this world without a gallant effort and you planted, nurtured, and groomed the seed that grew to replace your image and I hope you're proud.

My dad loved to sing and play the guitar. His favorite song was "Letter Edged in Black." This is why the cover is edged in black in his memory. Dad, may you be watching from above and singing along as this message circulates over the land. The verse "may the angels bear as witness" eases my heart knowing many may be spared such a dreadful experience.

My mother is still living and was rather staunch on morals, values, and virtues. This book comes due and part from her views and principles also instilled in me. She always used to say, "patience is a virtue."

Someone has to stand up and be blunt and stop beating around the bush. We work too hard for our money for it to be bilked away like this, so let the truth ring! You see, in a world laced with corruption and hypocrites, I still believe the truth will set you free.

MY FATHER, JUNIOR DALE SCHUELKE, FEBRUARY 10, 1926 – APRIL 14, 2009

What's the difference between God and a Lawyer?

God doesn't think he is a lawyer.

PREFACE

"Let the laws be clear, uniform, and precise; to interpret laws is almost always to corrupt them." —Voltaire

WE ALL NEED A GOOD LAUGH from time to time. No matter how bad any situation is, you have to find some release of energy in a positive light. You could say I've written one long joke of my own and I'm curious to see who laughs.

It's time for Americans to wake up and band together to address a fundamentally huge societal issue that has the average taxpayer feeling like they're being poached and pilfered by the most surprising branch of government; the branch that was, in fact, established to govern law and order—the judicial system. The truth is that we are living in a fairytale judicial system laced with fraud.

What is your perception of the reputation of today's judicial system and the individuals who take an oath to uphold the law? Do you think those individuals faithfully and honestly represent the Constitution generated by the Founding Fathers of this country, or do you think they have more of an interest for the love of money?

I believe I'm not alone in my assessment that many Americans are sick and tired of our judicial system, and those who profess to represent it, because the system is simply not consistent. Attorneys and lawyers call wrongful civil acts "tort," which are essentially unlawful and illegal doings, infringing on our freedoms and rights. But we see it demonstrated regularly that there are no "tort" standards and there is no equality of justice whatsoever for violations of our constitutional rights of liberty and freedom. Some get multimillion-dollar awards while other cases of similar harm receive no justice because of variations of attorney competencies and latitudes given by a judge's personal opinions. There simply aren't any standards or common sense in the system. Don't believe me? Someone buys a coffee, spills it on himself, and receives a landfall of money in damages, while someone else loses his life savings in the Enron scandal and receives nothing. I believe Americans are fed up with this nonsense and I'm part of that crowd.

I believe attorneys have worn out their welcome of the term "civil" litigation. Attorneys expect Americans to sit patiently, pay disproportion-ately liberal lawyer fees, live with unjust results, and remain quiet about it all. How did we graduate from the quick and many times painful but immediate justice of the old days of the West, when the law was either the local US Marshall, or it was worn around the waist in the form of a leather belt with a six shooter, to the multi-year-long legal battles with both sides generally losing and the attorneys winning?

Oh, today in modern justice though, we are civilized. We give our money freely to the attorneys and expect legal representation of our constitutional rights and we roll the dice and watch attorneys "practice" applying the law. I think it's a game . . . it's really no more than a game with a staged near-certain outcome. The gross variations of quality legal representation and a system devoid of standards for financial loss, let alone pain and suffering, is despicable, and "white collar crime" is literally of no more justice served with significance than a bad attorney joke. This might not mean anything until it happens to you . . . then it's too late and you're a victim, too.

Rogue attorneys have taken up the so-called legal profession to join a league of hypocrisy whose focus is to deceive and to bilk clients and society for the love of money, while becoming undiscerning to the principles and ethics of laws and liberties. Has the love for money become the sole underlying root of their motivation? If you believe this is possible, then at what level of infiltration into the public sector, business, and political world do you think attorneys with this mentality exist? I believe it exists at the highest office of the land, in the executive branch of our government . . . the infiltration is acute.

We've seen case after highly publicized case play out on TV. And we roll our eyes in disgust when the bad guy (or gal) gets off due to a technicality or an error. So how many more stunningly deceptive criminal attorney cases do Americans need to see before we realize the judicial system is breeding a litany group of frauds, hypocrites, conspirators, and outright liars?

Take, for example, the notorious attorney, the darling two-time presidential candidate John Edwards who was indicted on six felony charges, yet claimed he "did not break the law." The entire American society and political infrastructure and landscape should have had their belly full of notions about attorneys with Mr. Edwards' ill-fated art of swindling trickery, funneling nearly $1 million dollars of campaign contributions. He wrongfully took campaign finance monies for supporting his extramarital private love life with Rielle Hunter, her pregnancy with his child he didn't want anyone to know about, and the concealment of the truth of his sex tape. Mr. Edwards obviously expected someone else to bear the financial responsibility for his irresponsible actions. He obviously didn't think he should have to pay for this illegitimate child himself and expected someone with deep pockets to cover his mistake. Even the greatest of trickery artists can't hide the evidence of a human child with hoards of money forever. Even more astonishing is the notion that some attorneys were concerned that this event might cause Mr. Edwards, the devoted family man, to lose his license to be an attorney . . . and never be able to practice law again. This is a prime example of this kind of judicial background and "I'm above the law" rhetoric, and Americans need to take a hard look at the underlying cause of why this happens and why it is allowed to continue.

• • •

I come from a background of industrial manufacturing and I'm also a Commercial Pilot. My career involved applying the skills I learned from the University of Nebraska in Manufacturing Engineering with Industrial Plant Management expertise. It was my job on a daily basis to seek root causes of product and production failures and generate solutions with my available resources, which consisted of what I called the four M's: Man, Materials, Machines, and Methods. So whenever the human element contributed to the failure of a manufacturing process, I was able to directly dissect why the person was failing on the job.

There are many factors that contribute to failures but I always focused on first ensuring that adequate and proper training was completed and provided by the company, because that was our responsibility. Even though blame is cast all too unjustly and quickly in our society, I always made sure employees were given the benefit of the doubt because I like to stand up for the worker who provides goods and services we all utilize each and every day. Now, if that person commits sabotage to cause an operation to break or fail, that's a whole other human element you must, and I emphasize must, deal with immediately or that person can destruct and severely jeopardize an entire manufacturing organization and even bring it to its knees, such that everyone involved loses their jobs.

The bottom line is this: In manufacturing, you must take immediate action to address failures, or you are very possibly out of business overnight. There is absolutely no room for complacency or mediocrity.

Conversely, our society is currently tolerating a gross amount of injustice within attorney ethics and it needs to change—dramatically and immediately! I am simply applying some common sense and my analytical career skills to what happened to me within the judicial system. I didn't see it as rocket science. I am confident you will not see it as rocket science either. I am, however, amazed that literally no one is publicly touting and addressing this grossly huge and impactful judicial issue! Let's get with it, shall we? And by the way, judges aren't exempt here either. Judges are mere former attorneys who think they know it all best!

What do you call a lawyer gone bad?

A senator.

Speaking of senators, why is it that the notorious actor and former Senator Fred Thompson makes the national spot light as seen being paid to lobby for attorneys for unlimited caps on jury awards, which directly affects the bottom line an attorney takes home from the payoff? I don't recall any other victims' rights or proposed laws that Mr. Thompson has made any conscious effort to bolster for the betterment of an average crime afflicted victim, which he so proudly portrayed to fight for as a movie star and actor. Is it more for money and less about the concern for the American judicial system's victim, caring less about the outcome and restitution of the American swindled victim? Personally, I believe that's what it is the lion's share of the time.

POLITICS AND WHISKEY

Oh, can attorneys and senators put their own twists and slants on a topic for the occasion. In 1952, Armon M. Sweat, Jr., a member of the Texas House of Representatives, was asked about his position on whiskey. What follows is his exact answer (taken from the Political Archives of Texas):

> If you mean whiskey, the devil's brew, the poison scourge, the bloody monster that defiles innocence, dethrones reason, destroys the home, creates misery and poverty, yea, literally takes the bread from the mouths of little children; if you mean that evil drink that topples Christian men and women from the pinnacles of righteous and gracious living into the bottomless pit of degradation, shame, despair, helplessness, and hopelessness, then, my friend, I am opposed to it with every fiber of my being.
>
> However, if by whiskey you mean the oil of conversation, the philosophic wine, the elixir of life, the ale that is consumed when good fellows get together, that puts a song in their hearts and the warm glow of contentment in their eyes; if you mean Christmas cheer, the stimulating sip that puts a little spring in the step of an elderly gentleman on a frosty morning; if you mean that drink that enables man to magnify his joy, and to forget life's great tragedies and heartbreaks and sorrow; if you mean that drink, the sale of which pours into Texas treasuries untold millions of dollars each year, that provides tender care for our little crippled children, our blind, our deaf, our dumb, our pitifully aged and infirm, to build the finest highways, hospitals, universities, and community colleges in this nation, then my friend, I am absolutely, unequivocally in favor of it.

This is my position, and as always, I refuse to compromise on matters of principle.

I believe I could hardly find a better contrasting and contradictory example coming from a politician's mouth than that one.

But on the grand scale in our country, our society has been acutely victimized by the cunningly unscrupulous seduction of the law profession, and this American wholly believes that this is one of the most important underlying reasons why our Executive, Legislative, and Judicial politicians, largely made up of attorneys, can't agree on how and why it is necessary to cut federal spending, since they continue to demand to spend money this country doesn't have. We just don't have enough business savvy folks in politics to carry majority votes so fiscal irresponsibility rules the land.

I also fully believe that most attorneys don't care where money comes from; they just want to leach onto those who have it, suck all they can get, and let the hosts figure out how to produce it. How much more evidence do we need to see on the local and national stages to come to our senses? Why does it take a debt crisis threatening to shut down the Federal government for people to realize *our politicians would still get paid while our military personnel wouldn't?*

So who is to blame? "We the people" have let it happen. We're all to blame. If it's ever going to get any better, somebody has to first recognize the fundamental problem, expose it, and deal with it in a truly democratic system. Numbers can overpower what the love for money has bought in politics. We've just got to get with the program and this book is a start! If the mass of numbers needs something to talk about for Monday morning quarterbacking, then let the film roll.

Did you hear about the lawyer from Texas who was so big when he died that they couldn't find a coffin big enough to hold the body?

They gave him an enema and buried him in a shoebox.

INTRODUCTION

I'VE HEARD ENOUGH about how America has the greatest and best judicial system compared to all other countries on the face of this earth. I know I'm actually speaking for millions, yes millions, of Americans who have had very similar, if not exactly the same impression of attorneys and the highly ineffective judicial system.

We, in America, have over one million licensed attorneys doing their thing, whatever that thing is, and I believe not only millions of Americans believe the American judicial system is not only far from perfect, but that it is corrupt.

Citizens have had enough with the legal system's lack of integrity, lack of standards and uniformity, lack of justice, lack of common sense and demented concepts of tort, outrageous billing rates, and the transgression of our American judicial system from benevolence to evil. Oh, it's the world's greatest judicial system, depending on which side of the law you are on. If you're not on the right side, you'd better beware!

It's high time the truth be revealed; time to unmask and disclose the fraudulent and unethical actions by attorneys and lawyers who disgrace the judicial system with self-righteous acts of perversion. Then we can indeed apply some lessons learned, as one of them suggested, so as to, and I quote, "abate our motivations to demonize" those attorneys "whose actions, embroiled in conflict, tend to just leave us with a bad case of misunderstandings and a lack of knowledge of the process" . . . meaning the so-called legal process. In my personal dealings with attorneys and judges, it was expressingly stated that the average American citizen should learn to cast aside our hatred of our bad experiences with attorneys, the unjust legal system, and the crappy judicial process. He is right! And I think I have found a way to do it.

I just finished an over-eleven-years-long legal battle within the so-called judicial system, and I'll admit I was deceived for some time, but I started figuring out that I needed to pay closer attention because I became suspicious of some foul play.

I was defrauded by a group of chumps in a stock fraud scheme and then I believe I was defrauded by an attorney while attempting to search for justice. I failed to achieve justice in both cases, due to the most bizarre circumstances. So, I have taken it upon myself, rather than tuck this experience under the chin and proceed as if it never happened, to document the actual occurrences of what I believe was gross misconduct of those attorneys and judges. I profess what happened in my case wasn't just a bad case of misunderstandings and a lack of knowledge of the process, but rather outright intentional acts and gross miscarriages of justice within the legal system. And I'd like to share it with you.

I could have accepted an attorney's meager monitary compensation and offer of confidentiality and never published a word of this event, but then I would have lived my life knowing what I experienced and learned and knowing how I could have educated and warned thousands, if not millions, of unsuspecting Americans that there are actually attorneys like this out there . . . and kept quiet about it all. That, to me, would not be right and just. I wrestled with trying to put this aside and move on, but I just couldn't do it. I am compelled to educate and alert the public and I hope my story will benefit and safeguard naïve and unsuspecting Americans.

LAWYERS AND ALLIGATORS

Two alligators are sitting on the edge of a swamp. The small one turns to the big one and says, "I don't understand how you can be so much bigger than I am. We're the same age, we were the same size as kids ... I just don't get it."

"Well," says the big alligator, "what have you been eating?"

"Lawyers, same as you," replies the small alligator.

"Hmm. Well, where do you catch 'em?"

"Down at that law firm on the edge of the swamp."

"Same here. Hmm. How do you catch 'em?"

"Well, I crawl under a BMW and wait for someone to unlock the door. Then I jump out, bite 'em, shake the crap out of 'em, and eat 'em!"

"Ah!" says the big alligator, "I think I see your problem. See, by the time you get done shakin' the crap out of a lawyer, there's nothing left but lips and a briefcase."

CHAPTER 1:

BAMBOOZLED AND CHAPPED

YOU COULD SAY I was a little slow to catch on as to what was happening to me.

Back in the middle of the 1990s when the economy was slightly better, many folks were investing in the stock market. I was working sixty to ninety hours per week at my job and was making investments like many other Americans focusing on building retirement.

Then, the unthinkable happened. I had been investing in a West Coast company that claimed to be going public along with all the stock market dot-com performers when I realized the company, American Board Sports, (ABC Inc.) was just taking me along with 600–700 other investors for a financial joy ride. The company had been making all kinds of statements that they were securing sales contracts with big-name customers like Walmart and so on.

I made my first investment of just under $40,000 with this company in July of 1995. The company claimed to have purchase orders of over $500,000 from trade shows and was giving sales projections of $96,552,890 . . . yes that is $96 million in sales. That's quite a projection for a relatively new startup company. I was tickled to be on board as a shareholder.

Over the next two years, I made several more investments in this company as they cleverly offered option shares for those who could significantly invest more and contribute to their capitalization and financial requirements they claimed they needed to finish the process to enable their company to be publicly traded. The option shares were a mere piece of paper that stated you could purchase more shares of the company for around a $1 per share if the company went public, and if the stock price was $15–$20, the options would be worth a lot of money. They were touting their company with others that were hitting $40–$80 per share.

The company didn't go public in the time frame they said it would but they kept representing that they were still doing so well and, in fact, published an article in *Success* magazine in January of 1998, stating the company had netted $4 million dollars in revenue and had 36 employees. A smiling picture of the company's president Tom Carter was featured on the front cover of that month's addition of *Success* magazine. "Make millions while you play," was his motto!

As I said earlier, I was a little slow to figure out what was actually going on 2,000 miles away from where I was living and working, but finally in December of 1998, I made a trip to San Diego to get some answers as to just what was going on.

I flew out to San Diego to attend a share holders' meeting only to learn that the company's sales were not what they had said they were, and they were reverse-splitting the investors shares, meaning we were getting shafted. Not only that, the company announced they were no closer to going public with their stock and another group was coming in to handle capitalization procurement. The shareholders were not happy.

This was the same company who, earlier in January of the year, received *Success* magazine press for impressive revenues and making millions while you play. You see, the company claimed to be making sports board products—skateboards, surfboards, wakeboards, snowboards, and a host of associated clothing apparel.

Ironically, the company management wanted to vote on reelection of the current officers before dispelling the status of the company, to which I stood and objected. I asked to have the accounting balance sheets and quarterly reports visited before the vote of reelection of officers commenced. The CFO asked why I requested to change the order of their meeting and I explained that I believed the shareholders certainly would like to know how the current officers were performing before the shareholders casted their votes to reelect them. I simply stated that I thought it would be prudent to apprise the group of the current and actual status of the company. President Thomas N. Carter turned a little red when I made this request. Mr. Carter turned to his CFO Joseph Lindquist and asked if they could do that and Lindquist's face also turned a little red, but they agreed to oblige. I believe this only accomplished setting me as the real focus or target of a masterful fraud scheme.

Later that next year of 1999, I contacted an attorney to enforce Corporation laws of being able to obtain corporation minutes, bylaws, and specific management activity documents that I was entitled to as a shareholder of the company. My attorney sent the company a threatening letter stating if the company didn't provide copies of the documents I wanted, then they would be receiving the summons of a lawsuit and they would be paying the bill.

Well, this worked out real well. The company took in all this and back-doored me by going to our family stockbroker and heisting nearly one-quarter of a million dollars without my knowing it. Months passed and absolutely no documentation of the transaction was made by the company so when I found out, I was furious. I had no other choice than to ask the attorney to file a lawsuit for fraud, which he did.

I thought this was bad. But I also thought I would have no trouble proving the whole mess was one large fraud scheme, especially the last transaction. I thought the deceit was going to be so easily proved, even the attorney told me that once the checks were found to be cashed inside the company and the money was spent in a few days, the fraud would be established and a trial would not even be needed.

Little did I know at the time, my attorney had other ideas of how to handle the case for his benefit. I was a good client. I had been paying my attorney invoices up to near the time of the trial until I discovered what was going on. I ended up going into trial against the company and its associated defendants only to discover one of the most shameful presentations of my evidence was solely at the hands of my attorney who obtained critical evidence illegally that was subsequently barred from trial. In addition, a whole host of other gross actions eventually led me to pursue filing a lawsuit against my very same attorney for fraud, malpractice, malice, conversion, and unethical conduct. I followed my attorney's advice as any good client would be expected to, but I had been played to be a fool.

Yes, my attorney obtained proof that the company received the checks, deposited them, and quickly spent the money. He illegally obtained proof that one of the individuals involved also received checks, deposited them and spent the money, too. Yet, he continued with preparation for trial even though his actions pretty much ruined any chance we had of winning.

I had gone this far with the litigation against the company and defendants, and the attorney kept forming a new and better game plan that was to have a better ending result.

What transpired before, during, and in the aftermath of the underlying case of the ABC company with my attorney is just too bizarre not to expose to the public.

Why did the post office recall the new lawyer stamps?

Because people couldn't tell which side to spit on.

I dare say I'm not alone when it comes to be taken advantage of by an attorney and this book is a testament of just how deceptive an entire group of attorneys and judges can be to protect a charged comrade of serious infractions—more gut-wrenching and intense than any box-office thriller.

It's one thing to become a victim of fraud but it's quite another to feel like you have been defrauded by attorneys and when you file charges against an attorney and attempt to prosecute for fraud, deceit, malice, malpractice, conversion, and unethical conduct—you lose. You appeal in every court possible to you in this country and you still lose. You file your complaint with the governing authority that is supposed to regulate attorneys and you lose again but you can appeal and your appeal is denied—at the Supreme Court level in the United States.

Moreover, if you endeavor to do such a task, you're likely to find, as I did, that you will be told up front by judicial representatives that you are "entitled" to due process of law but if you try it, you're not really given a chance to be heard in front of a jury of personally selected and approved jurors to ensure an unbiased panel exists. Instead, you are ensnared in a court forum made up of attorneys, paid by the attorney you've charged with the crime.

Should anyone guess what the outcome was? I lost and the attorney won—big. He was awarded court costs and even awarded interest on the judgment, both prejudgment and post judgment. Interest even accrued while I appealed and filed a stay of execution on the collection of a judgment against me! I was subject to being found in contempt of court for not answering discovery collection questions while my appeal was commencing and the stay of execution was in place. As a matter of blatant fact, the attorney applied liens against my properties during the process and violated the release of lien laws and wanted absolutely no disclosure of this entire history to anyone except other attorneys and accountants as necessary.

How could it be that an attorney won defending himself from alleged fraud charges, but yet listed as an item #14 as a term of a proposed settlement agreement that he wanted "confidentiality." The terms are to be "strictly confidential" and that no party may refer to any of the terms of the agreement and either party may not "directly or indirectly disclose the terms" of the agreement "in any manner," "except to their attorneys and accountants, as reasonably necessary."

Specifically, why would an attorney have listed the following sentence, and proposed a settlement agreement, "The Schuelkes agree not to refer to Darren J. Quinn, either directly or indirectly, to anyone except their attorneys"? What possible reason could an attorney have to justify this action? Can you guess?

If it's not obvious, let me help you here. Although I was offered $700 at one point and time, I was not bought off, bullied, scared off, bribed, forced, or ordered to sign a "Confidentiality" statement in connection with the matters referred to here in this book—alas and hence, this book. Wouldn't all ethical attorneys enjoy a little free publicity and notoriety if their accomplishments were indeed above ground, ethical, and exemplary of what citizens assume the law profession is all about . . . instead of being "confidential"?

To date, these attorneys I encountered are all in good standing with the State Bar if you choose to check them out. One of them even wants to be a judge!

• • •

David Copperfield is a master of deception. I can't say I've ever figured out how he has done a single stunt. Some attorneys also consider themselves masters of deceit and deception and some practice, or should I say, tamper with evidence or manipulate evidence for their own personal self-gain.

I must declare, not all attorneys and judges are corrupt or intentional manipulators of evidence and I'm truly grateful for those straight shooting, ethical, honest, oath-abiding members who take pride in their roles in assisting citizens and businesses in the pursuit of legal justice. The judicial system was never intended to manipulate, tamper, curb, twist, and squelch the truth, and I believe honest attorneys and lawyers have to stand up and recognize their organization needs a different method of discipline to ensure homogenous integrity exists in the critical role they all play in our society. To this note, if you are a lawyer or a judge, I simply ask for your support to assist and clean up the rhetoric, as I'm confident a good percentage know exactly what I'm talking about here. Furthermore, I am extremely confident I am speaking for the majority of the American public and I am confident only good can come from this exposure for the betterment of society.

Why is the system so hard to use when trying to expose the truth? It's because the truth is so often discarded in the system because of technicalities, attorney incompetence, and outright mistakes. And judges allow it to happen. Should any attorney wonder why their profession is less than stellarly respected? Many attorneys enjoy the cesspool of cynical jokes about them. But most citizens of society would truly be embarrassed! For this reason, I believe attorneys deserve the reputation they seem to enjoy as a whole.

Do attorneys and judges have a restraining order on society to disable the questioning of authorities' bias rulings? If you have ever tried prosecuting an attorney for unethical conduct or fraud, you'll know what I mean by bias rulings. Chances are extremely high that you will not get a general jury trial against a charged attorney. Even if you haven't, are you familiar with how the process works? That's exactly where I'd like to provide some details and a good education.

The State Bar is the regulatory body that handles complaints against attorneys and judges. Just one main problem exists—they govern themselves. The State Bar suggests attorneys craft retainer agreements, to which the public doesn't get a chance to sit in on a jury panel to render a verdict, should you ever find yourself in disagreement with one of them. If you sign it, it becomes one mandated law of convenience, but not by coincidence! This is an elusive, trumped-up sham and gross form of injustice to you; attorneys have been evading the law in public, assassinating common sense, and certainly circumventing the Constitution of the United States of America. If you don't believe me, ask any attorney to provide you a copy of their retainer agreement and see how many contract retainer agreements list provisions for you to give up your right to a jury trial should any dispute with their fees arise—demanding arbitration. You might be surprised! This is an attorney's way of introducing you to the process called arbitration. Of course, this comes into play in the contract without any legal or real explanation of you giving up your rights. You may initially think this may be alright if you just have a fee dispute, but what if you are defrauded by your attorney? Regardless of the extent of an attorney's crime, you lose your Constitutional right to a public jury trial! It's a snaky and deceitful tactic attorneys like to use against you right from the start, and certainly before you realize just how corrupt they can be and get away with it.

• • •

It seems that there is actually a dual standard of justice and prosecution for attorneys and judges versus all other citizens who commit crimes. Attorneys and even judges have been grossly abusing the "conflict of interest" rules and concept to the point that they sit in on their own private arbitration/jury panels to render verdict decisions, in lieu of a host of local collectively chosen unbiased nonjudicial citizens.

Attorneys have gone too far in abusing this conflict of interest concept, and a major house cleaning and reform is in order, but is America too complacent and in too much of a nauseated state to even care? Year after year, decade after decade, we have allowed the thought and act of telling a lie to progress a little too far in our modern-day society. If you believe in the old cliché "give someone an inch and they will take a foot," then you'd likely agree that there is a possibility we have allowed the giving of a few too many inches of our rights and liberties in this country. A lot of it boils down to expectations, doesn't it?

If you hire an attorney to represent you, what level of service do you expect? You should expect error-free service in interpreting and applying the laws of the land for the rates attorneys charge, and you shouldn't be tolerant of some errors and mistakes. If an attorney does make mistakes, how many should you allow before you should be concerned or justifiably disgruntled and eventually take some sort of action? What if the mistake affects the outcome of your case? If the attorney is unwilling to correct the mistake or is unable to, you are faced with limited options. What should the judge involved do? Wouldn't you think that the judicial system ought to be an icon of perfection instead of a horrific disgrace of insubordination when it comes to interpreting and applying the laws of the land without stupendous errors and mistakes? What excuse do they have to justify incompetence when they charge the rates they all charge? The system isn't perfect. Is that it?

The liberty bell in Philadelphia has a crack in it. I've been there and a plaque states the crack represents the fact that some injustices do get through the system . . . I just never realized just how big and wide open that crack is until it came to needing the system myself. I was mortified at the lack of justice in this country and our system.

You may be amazed at what standards exist and how attorneys rate themselves in light of the rates they charge. The Rules of Professional Conduct standards and how they interpret and apply them to themselves as attorneys and lawyers (according to one of them who professes to be a seasoned veteran) are the most pitiful standards you could ever expect from a group who charges as though they are above the average citizen—so far that we as peasants aren't even high enough to be recognized on the food chain of organisms . . . more like scum. (Seems to me that many times the feelings are mutual.) Their standards are a disgrace to humanity, let alone members of the judicial system! You would expect something higher to reflect the outrageous compensation rates, but it is exactly the opposite.

During their time, Orville and Wilbur Wright didn't have the skills, resources, and money to sit down and design a model 747-400 Boeing aircraft right out of the hopper because it just wasn't possible. But yet, flight did evolve. Aircrafts evolved through decades of design, engineering, utilization, failures, crashes, lessons learned, and redesigning of the principle aircraft itself, and the system has continued to produce safer and more efficient aircrafts.

Similarly, but to the opposite degradation of effect, attorneys have selfishly, case after case, learned from their mistakes over time and lobbied for continual law changes for themselves, in which the populous has been uninvolved until we no longer have a clue what our rights are.

I believe this is a fundamental downfall of our modern society and we're not talking about it. What's worse is that this dubious cunning mentality is entrenched rock solidly in today's politics.

If you want a laugh, check the State Bar in your state and review how many complaints have been filed against attorneys and see what percentage get any action taken against an attorney. The results will shock you. Moreover, seek to understand who reviews those complaints and renders the response. The public is uninvolved! The fox is indeed guarding the hen house!

• • •

Thankfully, in my case, the attorney made one specific tactical mistake and miscalculation in dealing with me: He hired and paid a court recorder to sit in on our hearing. I simply figured that a turnabout play ought to be fair game. I summonsed this recorder to transcribe the hearing and paid her to give me a copy of the hearing. This, I'll dare say, is one move the attorney wished he'd never done. Because of this, I can provide you with the facts of their statements and responses to a whole host of my alleged fraud and unethical conduct charges. You will see first-hand what I was up against and you can be the judge to determine what should have happened. Attorneys love the game of making litigants look like they're lying, so why not turn the table with factual evidence and play the game back to show them lying?

We need to educate ourselves, form a game plan, and start initiating common sense democratic efforts of our own. I have some ideas starting with retainer agreements, the contractual agreement you sign with an attorney. Let's stop signing their existing proposed agreements for many reasons, including that they state they simply cannot guarantee you a result of their service, and insist they insert a clause something like this first:

> I solemnly swear or solemnly and sincerely affirm, as the case may be, that I will do nothing dishonest, and will not knowingly allow anything dishonest to be done in court, and that I will inform the court of any dishonesty of which I have knowledge; that I will not knowingly maintain or assist in maintaining any cause of action that is false or unlawful; that I will not obstruct any cause of action for personal gain or malice; but that I will efficiently exercise the office of attorney, in any court in which I may practice, without undue delays, according to the best of my learning and judgment, faithfully, to both my client and the court; so help me God or upon penalty of perjury; and I agree to abide by the Rules of Professional Conduct as provided by the American State Bar, and I will freely submit to civil or criminal prosecution in front of a public jury should my integrity ever become questioned.

I don't know about you, but I would also like every attorney to include a personal signed copy of their oath of their profession along with their retainer agreement before commencing legal representation.

Maybe we could better live with their results after we see them perform with competent legal and ethical behavior, according to the new clause. We might even be in a better mood to pay the bill, regardless of the result!

How much longer do we Americans need to go and how many cases and case examples do we all need to see to recognize that we have a lame duck branch of our government that needs to be woken up and overhauled? Let's just not sit on our laurels and wait until each and every one of us has been had by one of the million or so unscrupulous scoundrels. Let's shake off the numbness, wake up, and take some serious action. It starts right here!

So, the next time you step into a ballot box for any public figure position and place an "X" for an attorney or lawyer, hopefully you will have the knowledge, wisdom, and good judgment to truly know who you are casting your constitutional power for and what repercussions may well result!

FAIR AND SQUARE

Taking his seat in chambers, the judge faced the opposing lawyers. "I have been presented by both of you with a bribe," the judge began. Both lawyers squirmed uncomfortably.

"You, Attorney Leoni, gave me $15,000. And you, Attorney Campos, gave me $10,000."

The judge reached in his pocket and pulled out a check, which he handed to Leoni.

"Now, then, I'm returning $5,000, and we are going to decide this case solely on its merits."

CHAPTER 2:

IT WOULD HAVE BEEN NICE

IF ONLY THE JUDGE would have made the attorney do his ethical and legal job, this book would have most likely never been written. And, I'd never have this story to tell you. So what inept, unethical conduct could my attorney, Mr. Darren J. Quinn, have ever done for me to become upset with him? Let's see.

It's your first jury trial. You are the plaintiff and you look forward to getting your evidence against the fraudulent defendants out in front of the judge and jury. But your attorney dismays the judge right from the very start. You learn not only did your attorney sandbag a critical procedural matter for eleven months, but your attorney now intends to use this previous procedural ruling, which would bar the defendants from providing any testimony . . . and the judge won't allow it. You are screwed from the start.

That's exactly what happened to me. Instead of my attorney filing a motion for the judge to rule based on the fact the defendants would not answer discovery questions, my attorney decided to proceed with the expensive process of preparing for a full-blown trial and draging me into it. Then at trial, my attorney expected the judge to disbar the defendants from being able to testify, due to the judge's ruling eleven months prior. It seemed like I had found my attorney under a rock instead of on the 19th floor of a downtown San Diego office building.

At trial, the judge took off his glasses and was not impressed. My attorney sought to enter evidence on one of the defendants, which he said was the strongest claim, and the defense attorney claimed the evidence was obtained illegally. I learned right from the start that the judge wouldn't allow the evidence to be introduced in the trial at all. The attorney unlawfully obtained one of the defendants' bank account documents without providing notice first. The judge didn't do anything about this either! Incredible! There certainly were no repercussions to my attorney, only to me.

If that wasn't enough to choke me up, after the judge ruled against my attorney's tricky little attempt to disbar the defendants' evidence, the judge said he needed to see some evidence and my attorney explained he was really not ready because the computer he was planning on using had a hard drive crash and it would take him a few minutes to prepare the first piece of evidence on a new computer. Unfortunately, this was only a prelude of incompetence of what was to come during trial.

"Lawyers are the only persons in whom ignorance of the law is not punished." —Jeremy Bentham

---

Oh, can an attorney play with your case! My case went from: it won't be necessary to have a trial once the evidence of the money trail is determined and bank copies have been obtained, to: here we go to a full-blown trial with a jury. Only too late in the game did I realize I'd been played for the benefit of huge legal fees.

My fraud case was focused on a company and four defendants. One defendant, not directly associated with the company, did not appear at trial, so that left three to defend themselves.

It was on a Monday morning September 16, 2002. Again, it was our first day at trial. The jury had not been brought in yet and the attorneys and the judge were discussing some matters.

Mr. Quinn submitted paperwork showing that the defending company was a "suspended" corporation because the company had not filed their corporation paperwork, which is legally required to be a corporation in good standing, and therefore the company was unable to defend itself in trial. The defense attorney stated, "If the court is inclined to deny my motion, for the record, I would request a continuance until A.B.C. Co. can conform to the statute. It would be in the interests of justice at a trial on the merits to not have an administerial act interfere with the due process rights of the real party in interest."

Basically, the defense attorney was asking for an extension of time to take care of this problem with the paperwork, which is a rather routine task so that the company could defend itself in the lawsuit. I guarantee that this wasn't the first time in history in a court of law that an "administerial act" could possibly interfere or impact due process of law.

I'd like you to take notice of this action by the defense attorney and remember how he asks the judge for mercy as his actions impacted the ability of the company to defend itself at trial. Compare this defense attorney to my attorney's actions and take note as to how my attorney's actions impacted the outcome of my lawsuit.

Interestingly, the judge took a hard stance on the law and ruled that the company could not defend itself and it looked like Mr. Quinn had won a huge part of the case right from the start.

So it was established that the defending company ABC was defaulted by a technicality and was guilty as charged. The defendants had lost a major chunk of their case. As our case was filed against both the company and the individuals who committed the crime, who wouldn't have been ecstatic right now? With the company guilty by default, where do you think that left the individual defendants with respect to the charges against them? One might conclude we were going to get a judgment against the company to at least get our money back, right? Wrong.

> The presiding judge, Vincent P. DiFiglia, asks my attorney, "Where do we go from here?"

> My attorney, Mr. Quinn: "Where do we go from here?"

> Judge DiFiglia: "Tell me."

> Mr. Quinn: "To trial, your honor."

> Judge DiFiglia: "Trial against whom?"

> Mr. Quinn: "Trial against the individuals."

Great. Now the judge is chastising my attorney.

Mr. Quinn could have filed the paperwork and closed the case—all before this trial. I could have received a judgment against the company for all my damages, losses, and interest on my monies. If you stop and think about it, if it is so determined that the company is guilty of the charges of fraud against it, then how are the defendants going to prove otherwise? Instead, Mr. Quinn wanted to continue to try the case against the individuals.

If the judge was puzzled, then it should have been no wonder why I was puzzled, too.

As my attorney proceeded, he dug himself a hole that even the judge couldn't cover up.

Only moments later after this exchange, the judge addresses Mr. Quinn and asks,

> Judge DiFiglia: "Mr. Quinn, is this your first trial, by any chance?"
>
> Mr. Quinn: "No, your honor."
>
> Judge DiFiglia: "Second? Third? What?"
>
> Mr. Quinn: "Jury trial or court? Ninth, tenth."
>
> Judge DiFiglia: "Ninth, tenth jury trial."
>
> Mr. Quinn: "No, not jury trial. Six jury trials."

This is a great way for your trial to start, with the judge hazing your attorney and establishing the fact that I hadn't hired a real seasoned trial attorney. I was thrilled to learn that Mr. Quinn had not conducted many trials and developed expertise in handling himself professionally in the courtroom! There was one incompetent example after another that my attorney, Mr. Quinn, just seemed to be out to lunch when it came to practicing law and the judge was quick to point it out for all of us present.

Maybe the judge was trying to tell me indirectly that I hadn't paid enough money for a good attorney.

What is the definition of a jury?

A jury consists of twelve people chosen to decide who has the best lawyer.

It was time for the defense attorney to show some of his stuff. His name was Kennan E. Kaeder. I'll have to say, for being in the position the defendants were in, this defense attorney was older, far more seasoned than Mr. Quinn, and far better prepared to defend his clients based on his court room experience. And it definitely showed. The defense attorney chewed up Mr. Quinn and made him look like chunky peanut butter. Here's one example of what the defense attorney did.

The defense attorney asserted that our claims should be denied based on the statute of limitations laws and Judge DiFiglia asked Mr. Quinn, "Well, what would preclude them from being a bar to some of them?"

Statute of limitations applies to the length of time the law gives you to file a lawsuit against someone or a company. If you don't file a lawsuit typically in one year after the matter transpires, the wonderful laws of the United States judicial system deny you to ever file a lawsuit, period, and you are out of luck to prosecute or litigate anything on the matter. Isn't this a wonderful law? If you are on the side of the crooks, the statute of limitations works great. If you are on the getting taken side, our laws work against you and can ultimately ban you from filing a suit forever . . . the crooks are scott-free forever!

Mr. Quinn answered, "What would preclude them on claims that can be equitably tolled or stopped for fraudulent concealment? The statute would not run on those."

Judge DiFiglia responded, "You know, it would have been nice if we had gotten maybe a motion for summary judgment sometime ago or something to that nature."

How about that! Mr. Quinn argues that if I was defrauded, there would not be any such time constraint of filing the lawsuit and that all my investments would be legitimate to claim in the lawsuit. The judge then comments on how nice it would have been if my attorney had followed normal legal lawsuit protocol and filed a procedural motion for the judge to rule on so we didn't have to go to trial. But no. Mr. Quinn preferred to proceed on into trial unnecessarily.

It didn't seem to help that the judge also stated, "This case has been marked by delay and noncompliance by the defendants in this case from day one," and "the way this case is proceeding is not the most organized in the world," and "educating this court with respect to law which I am not familiar with has not been up to standards." I kept thinking about the judge's statement: *"it would have been nice."* Afterall, to whose liking does delay and noncompliance benefit? Is it Mr. Quinn's or mine? I'll assume you can figure this one out on your own. Just remember, time is money.

In the next few minutes of trial, Mr. Quinn's actions exposed the bomb he intended to drop on both the judge and the defense, a "sandbagged" (term used by the defense attorney to describe the unethical tactic of purposefully delaying the exposure of evidence) motion eleven months prior. Mr. Quinn sat on an order by the judge, which Mr. Quinn should have acted upon two weeks after the judge ruled, but Mr. Quinn didn't. The defendants were ordered to provide answers to questions asked by Mr. Quinn.

The judge asked Mr. Quinn: "Was the notice of the court's ruling sent to Mr. Kaeder (the defense attorney)?"

Mr. Quinn answered: "I did not do a formal notice." (Remember this answer!)

This is an attorney caught not communicating within the judicial system. The case should have been closed and we should have been attempting to collect from the guilty party. But instead, we've been playing a game of hide-and-go-seek with evidence. It became blatantly obvious that we should not have even been in trial that day if my attorney had done his job. Was Mr. Quinn stupid, sloppy, or just interested in playing games with my case? I believe he intended it this way.

First, Mr. Quinn intentionally failed to act on the judge's order compelling the defendants to answer Mr. Quinn's questions and then intentionally failed to provide proper communication to the defense attorney on the matter at hand . . . or was somebody lying? In the interest of realistic justice, how and why did both Judge DiFiglia and Mr. Quinn allow this to happen? The resulting consequences of this delay tactic dramatically both compromised and impacted my case's outcome beyond belief. I lost the capability of using critical evidence in my case, instead of being in a position of collecting against the company. Now I started seeing and smelling some of the real rotten fruit. You see, the motion was a simple motion to compel or order the defendants to answer some discovery questions Mr. Quinn was lawfully entitled to ask the defendants, like "Did you take the plaintiff's money?" and "Did you commit fraud?" If you commited fraud and defrauded a quarter of a million dollars from someone, would you want to answer questions under oath that you commited fraud? Obviously, these defendants didn't want to either!

Almost a year prior, on October 26, 2001, the judge had given the defendants fourteen days to answer all of the discovery questions or they would be in violation of this order. But it didn't happen. The defendants did, in fact, not answer those questions within the next fourteen days, as ordered by the court.

I'm no attorney and you don't have to be one to understand this, but I learned that the normal protocol by an attorney would be to then file what Judge DiFiglia called a "motion for summary judgment against the unanswering defendants." This motion would give the judge the power to render a ruling against the defendants called a "default judgment." If a defendant does not cooperate with the lawsuit, then the judge is entitled to grant a judgment in your favor. That's what Mr. Quinn should have done but he did not. (So, for all you criminals, if you want to know how to beat the system, don't answer the interrogatory questions and hope you have an opposing attorney like Mr. Quinn who won't press judicial process so you don't have to tell the truth, or for that matter, tell a lie and worry about ever getting caught doing it!)

By any attorney's standards, including ethics and morals, Mr. Quinn just thought he was above it all. Mr. Quinn opted not to obey or see to it that Judge DiFiglia's order was carried out. Rather, he took it upon himself to let the scoundrels off the hook and marched onward knowing full well the defendants who took the money never had to comply with the law and instead wanted to play a game of his own.

Mr. Quinn filed our original lawsuit on March 22, 2001. Basic math says that if fourteen days after October 26, 2001, Mr. Quinn had filed a motion for summary judgment instead of sandbagging my case, we likely would have had a judgment against everyone in the month of November of 2001. From March to November is eight months, which is still not very expedient but that would have been acceptable to me and likely to most citizens, I believe, in this kind of a case.

So why didn't Mr. Quinn file a motion for summary judgment? Why did he sit on the judge's order for eleven months until the first day of trial? Why didn't he send a formal notice to the defense attorney? Do you suppose Mr. Quinn just wanted to take 13 to 14 depositions and charge me for them? Do you suppose Mr. Quinn just wanted to rack up more discovery attorney fees and then add more trial preparation fees? Whatever the reason, I believe this was a violation of an existing conduct rule in the Rules of Professional Conduct Rule 5-200 Trial Conduct (B) that states, "In presenting a matter to a tribunal, a member: shall not intentionally mislead the judge, judicial officer, or jury ... "

I believe this behavior also violated the Rule 3-110 Failing to Act Competently (A), which states, "A member shall not intentionally, recklessly, or repeatedly fail to perform legal services with competence." I believe Mr. Quinn knew full well what he was doing and I believe he sandbagged my case intentionally.

Have you heard about the lawyer's word processor?

No matter what font you select, everything comes out in fine print.

Sadly, here we were, the first day of trial making these discoveries. Mr. Quinn's hidden schemes were coming out on the table. Did this impact the case? Absolutely. The records show Mr. Quinn and Judge DiFiglia had many words about this action of Mr. Quinn's, and there were numerous "side bars" where the judge called both attorneys to the bench for private discussions that I'll never know the details of.

Mr. Quinn had prepared a motion called a "Plaintiffs Trial Brief RE: Admitted Requests for Admission Are Conclusively Established" dated for the first day of trial, September 16, 2001, 9:00 a.m., and submitted it to the judge to rule on. This brief included two exhibits: #93 and #94, which would have denied two of the four defendants the chance to even testify and defend themselves individually—Joe Lindquist and Tom Carter. These two knew they were guilty and wouldn't answer any of the questions about committing fraud, and yet Mr. Quinn let them off the hook by not making them answer the questions. As far as the third defendant in the courtroom that day, John Cole, Mr. Quinn thought he had a slam dunk with Mr. Cole's bank checks that Mr. Quinn obtained—illegally.

Oh, what a glorious day in court this would have been for Mr. Quinn if this all worked out the way he had planned. The defendants would not have been able to testify, supply any evidence, and defend themselves in any way, shape, or form. Mr. Quinn wanted the judge to rule on a motion brief he filed that very morning that read, "any contrary evidence should be disregarded" by the court. Therefore, defendants Mr. Thomas N. Carter and Joseph Lindquist would be guilty as charged in the lawsuit and liable for financial damages.

But to no surprise regarding this submission, the judge wasn't happy. In fact, he said since we'd come this far, he wanted to see some evidence and wasn't going to rule at that time on evidentiary objections. The judge also asked to have the jury panel brought in the courtroom and proceed with getting the trial underway.

Is this the standard of care you would like to see from your attorney representing you in any legal matter? I'm going to show you later just what the judge had to say about this!

I can assure you, Mr. Quinn didn't care at the time to elaborate to me as to what was happening because I'm figuring his little scheme was falling through the cracks and he was scrambling to figure out how he was going to salvage the case.

In addition and to add insult to injury, before the jury was brought in, Mr. Quinn agreed to stipulate dropping our Federal Securities law claims on claims that were likely to fail at trial due to being subject to statute laws of limitations, which the defense attorney was raising. Sadly, I had no say in this; this conversation was between the judge and the attorneys.

If the lawful time allowed had passed to sue the company and these jokers, then what was the purpose of my attorney Mr. Quinn listing the barred claims in the lawsuit?

Was the whole attorney cost of trial preparation for these claims ever a waste of attorney fees! Mr. Quinn charged me dearly for filing these claims initially and then dropped them like a hot potato the first day of trial. We had both Federal and State Securities law claims in our lawsuit against the defendants that Mr. Quinn included in our filing. Now we were only left with State law violation claims.

If you catch the drift here, you might deduce that I'd been played in a game of chess . . . except I was just a pawn and my claims were worth about as much value. Mr. Quinn obviously filed the lawsuit stating Federal Security laws had been violated. Mr. Quinn obviously researched the laws and charged me for that; called and spoke with me about it and charged me for that; wrote the claim in the filed complaint of the lawsuit and charged me for that; discussed this with Mr. Kaeder on several occasions and charged me for that; generated an invoice and charged me for that; traveled to court to argue this in front of the judge and defense attorney and charged me for that; and decided to simplify the case in my presence and in the presence of the judge and charged me for that. If I missed any charges I was charged, I'm sorry for that.

I just have to ask, why do attorneys do this sort of thing? Why do they trump up charges in your case and just drop them like they were no longer important or no longer serve any purpose other than to run up a monstrous attorney bill? Do they think Americans think this is just another kind of professional sporting event individuals can afford to fund?

To me, one of two things happened here: Either Mr. Quinn really didn't understand the Federal Securities laws as he represented to me that he did, or Mr. Quinn realized he couldn't pull a rabbit out of a hat in front of the judge. I believe Mr. Quinn finally realized his illegal stunt of obtaining Mr. Cole's checks wouldn't work and that he lost my greatest claim on the "dirtiest defendant" when he screwed up by not serving the notice to the defendant. Either way, I paid a small fortune for Mr. Quinn's education and I received absolutely no benefit from it, but sure, pure, and expensive embarrassment.

One of the next notable events that morning was right at the opening of trial with the jury present. Mr. Quinn stated, "I had somewhat of a hectic morning on my laptop. The hard drive crashed. I had to borrow a laptop, and I think I now have it going, but I need two minutes to prepare one exhibit, to show the jury for opening, if I may." There were no hard copy binders of the evidence for any of us—the judge, the defendants, or the jury. My case was an experiment with Mr. Quinn. A new software called Sanctions II had recently come out, which enables attorneys to project a case from right off a laptop computer onto a projector and big screen. I was a guinea pig for Mr. Quinn and unfortunately, this experiment backfired.

In our opening argument, Mr. Quinn tells the jury that this case involves fraud and that, "the testimony is going to show there is a picture of fraud. This is a picture of my client's money being literally taken . . . This is a stock fraud case . . . Your honor, I apologize for the computer problems. I was planning on having everything today, but my hard drive crashed, and so this is a new computer."

Can you imagine being on a jury waiting to see a "picture" of the fraud? My attorney just mislead the jury because there was never any such surveilance or security camera tape or picture to show the jury! If I were a juror, that's what I would have expected. Mr. Quinn couldn't even professionally articulate or speak to the jury without giving them a false sense of my case evidence. He should have simply said he was going to put up the evidence on a projection screen instead of passing out copies of the documents of the evidence . . . except he didn't have the copies prepared just in case there was a mishap.

Mr. Quinn is apologizing to the judge for his misshap while my evidence is somewhere in computer crashland and Mr. Quinn is having a hard time showing this "picture" on the wall for everybody to see.

This is what Mr. Quinn was planning on using to present my case evidence to the judge and the jury. Am I just supposed to accept an apology for the computer problem? This is the inability of my attorney to present my evidence here! Mr. Quinn also tells the jury about the specific current condition of the company, "The revenues the last couple of quarters were zero" . . . and we are suing a company that is basically not operating and making any money for at least the last six months! Are we beating a dead horse? We'll see.

As the trial progressed, I about flipped when the defense attorney raised issue with Mr. Quinn attempting to enter evidence on one of the three defendants, which involved a bank account. Mr. Quinn had subpoenaed a Nevada bank account showing checks coming in and out. I would call it evidence of the money-laundering scheme. How ironic that the defense attorney objected to this evidence being entered before the jury, because he claimed Mr. Quinn obtained this evidence illegally. Why?

Mr. Kaeder informed the judge that Mr. Quinn had, in fact, not served or issued his client with a Notice of Privacy Right action and therefore the evidence was obtained illegally. Mr. Kaeder even admitted two of the defendants names were "all over these checks." Mr. Quinn had copies of the checks in his possession right there . . . at trial. But the judge ruled we could not use them.

That's real justice when the defendant testified in a deposition that he knew nothing about this Nevada bank account yet we had a copy of one particular check the defendant exchanged with the company charged, regarding our fraudulent transaction, and yet we couldn't use it to prove any such connection. Thank you very much, Mr. Quinn.

Just weeks before the scheduled trial, Mr. Quinn informed me in an e-mail that "I got the Bank of XXX documents in today. John Albert Cole, one of the defendants, was a signatory for Pacific Management. We can use the Bank of XXX records at trial. I take back my statement a day or so ago that your case was weakest against John Cole. He is now directly tied to the dirtiest of them all (Timothy J. Connor) on the strongest claim." Boy, was I excited the evidence was finally obtained . . . except now that we're at trial, we can't use it.

Again, Mr. Cole testified in a deposition months before the trial that he did not recognize this name of the company he was a signatory for, and claimed he had only heard of it. Mr. Quinn had in his possession the discovery documents from this company that showed Mr. Cole had signed a statement on December 5, 2001, to have all his pay for his fees to be directed to this Pacific Management company. His signature matched perfectly and there was no doubt in all our minds he was lying and we should have been easily able to link him to the fraud but could not . . . thanks to Mr. Quinn's incompetent and unlawful actions. Did it affect the results of the case? Far beyond belief!

Mr. Quinn called Mr. Cole to the witness stand and only, and I repeat only, asked him to state all the positions he held at the company and the dates, and "Did you ever become aware of any attempt by Dennis Schuelke to replace any of the management at the Company?"

Mr. Cole answered, "No."

Mr. Quinn: "No further questions."

Judge DiFiglia: "Thank you Mr. Cole. You may step down."

What? You may step down after asking the "dirtiest of them all," one question? What did this accomplish? What about the statement Mr. Quinn expressed so surely that we could use the Bank of XXX documents at trial since Mr. Cole was tied to the dirtiest of them all? Why didn't Mr. Quinn ask him something pertaining to his connection with the fraud? I never got Mr. Quinn to tell me. I don't believe Mr. Quinn even knew.

At least he knew he had his concealed bomb that could right any wrong: exhibits #93 and #94, so Mr. Quinn made his next move.

> Mr. Quinn: "Just a ministerial matter, plaintiffs move exhibits 93 and 94 into evidence."

These two exhibits were assumed-to-be-guilty answers to those unanswered questions by the defendants mentioned earlier. It was Mr. Quinn's slam-dunk approach.

The judge agreed with Mr. Kaeder that this would be dealt with outside the presence of the jury. How ironic, the judge would not allow any discussion in front of the jury about the fact the defendants did not answer our questions about taking my money, committing fraud, etc., and the fact that the defendants would not answer these questions when the case was initially filed a year earlier, yet, they are here in the courtroom today to attempt to defend themselves. No, we wouldn't want the jury to see that the judge and the attorneys had been playing games with the evidence; we wouldn't want the jury to see and hear the truth as to what actually happened, would we? No, let's conceal the truth at all cost to save face of the judge and attorneys while we screw the victim's case!

After the jury leaves, Judge DiFiglia removes his glasses and states:

> There was no motion to set aside the court's ruling on that with respect to … the admissions until the day of trial; and as I've indicated before gentlemen, I've got the paucity of law on this case. I've never been faced with this situation. Fifteen years on the bench, I've never been faced with this situation.
>
> And what we have is we've got a great deal of evidence that there was absolutely no fraud, that there was absolutely no detrimental reliance, and

then we have these [the two exhibits 93 and 94 which Mr. Quinn drafted stating the defendants admit to commiting fraud].

And, essentially, it allows this case to go by default, I suppose, unless the jury disregards the admissions.

But I don't know . . . you know, go home and do some research and tell me how to get out of this dilemma. I don't know.

Is it a miscarriage of justice? You're absolutely right. The question is whether I have the power to set it aside.

Mr. Quinn has just set forth a situation of judicial disgrace—attempting to nail the defendants of fraud and yet can't substantiate the claim with the hard evidence.

In the courtroom of supposedly two professional attorneys, one attempts to pull a tactical ploy back over on the judge, defense attorney, and the jury (my lawyer, Mr. Quinn), and the other attorney acts as though he is ignorant and didn't know about the court order (the defense attorney, Mr. Kaeder) . . . yet this is what my attorney is banking on for me to win my case. The judge calls the predicament a miscarriage of justice. The judge was right but didn't exercise his power to do the right thing judicially to address it. Rather than rule on the oversight by the mess of the matter, the judge refused to rule on it at all because he knew the defense attorney would take the fall on his "sword." The judge chose to let the plaintiff (me) take the hit for this disastrous monstrosity.

This is why in America, we more often claim judges "sit" on the bench rather than preside over the case and actually demonstrate superior or wise intellect. This instance shows the real and truly pathetic capability and power of an American judge.

Judge DiFiglia stated prior in the hearing:

> It is a maxim of law that, if the attorney falls on his sword, that . . . the court must rule. It is impossible, in view of the fact you were in the courtroom, the ruling was announced in the courtroom, to . . . to accept that you just missed it, Mr. Kaeder. And it's again, a case of first impressions. So much in this litigation has been . . . if I'm wrong, I'm wrong, but it does not constitute, in my mind, the neglect of counsel that I believe calls for relief . . .

Judge DiFiglia makes the case for himself: He just can't make up his mind to make an appropriate judicial ruling based on the incompetence and neglect of the defense attorney . . . even though it's the law—a maxim of law! Can you see the game being played here? The defense attorney claims ignorance to the judge's order and the judge is torn on what to do.

So if you're keeping count: The defense attorney whines that he just missed and was unaware of the judge's motion months ago to compel his defending clients to answer those fraud charged questions; Mr. Quinn pulls an unethical circus act of not informing either Judge DiFiglia or Mr. Kaeder of this vitally important unanswered order by the court; Mr. Kaeder cries for relief of insubordination; and Judge DiFiglia postures and threatens the defense attorney but won't follow through with the crucifixion.

I'm in disbelief in what I'm seeing before my very eyes. Lord, where did these jokers come from? And most surprising is why the judge isn't threatening Mr. Quinn for setting up this circus stunt to begin with! Why isn't Judge DiFiglia all over Mr. Quinn? I'm going to take the fall, while everybody gets paid out of my pocket . . . now that's justice!

So even though we had proof of fraud, since my attorney committed unlawful acts, I was the one to suffer the consequences! Obviously this impacted the case in a big way. You can see Judge DiFiglia certainly wasn't impressed either. Do you suppose Judge DiFiglia was a little slow to catch on to what was happening, just like I was?

Through this, what I call a fairyland laced with fraud, Mr. Quinn wanted me to take the stand as a witness during the trial. Once the defense had eliminated the harshest of fraud evidence by successfully calling out Mr. Quinn's illegal actions in obtaining bank documents and that Mr. Quinn was having a little trouble with accessing my evidence, the defense attorney had a field day with me and my testimony. He wanted me to show him where the fraud was! The defense attorney brought up a pile of papers stacked approximately 5–6 inches high, all loose and unbound and certainly not in any type of binder. I had never even seen this pile before the trial. Yes, it was communications paperwork I had received from this company, but it wasn't indexed, tabulated, or organized whatsoever! Besides, there was a whole lot more evidence to the case than just what the lying company sent me. The defense wanted me to expose the fraud we filed our claim about, having never seen the stack of papers before and with no time to examine the papers.

Mr. Quinn instructed me not to bring up any claims regarding those that had happened more than one year prior because the defense attorney would quickly bar them on grounds of statute of limitations, and you saw what happened with respect to our strongest fraud claim, Mr. Cole.

Also, Mr. Quinn told me before the trial that all the evidence was going to be entered from his computer using a new software called Sanctions II which he would put on an overhead projector for the trial attendees to see. He was going to try it out on this case for the first time in his life and you saw how that turned out.

Mr. Quinn said he had to borrow a friend's computer the night before the first day of trial in an attempt to salvage the concept of using the new software. How much evidence was lost and never utilized, I'll never know. I do know one thing . . . not one bit of evidence was utilized from all those depositions Mr. Quinn took. There was just one more problem—I didn't have access to the projector screen when I was on the stand. That created a slight difficulty. I stared at Mr. Quinn while I was on the stand and he looked back at me like a spooked and spanked jackal.

To this day, Mr. Quinn blames me for this insidious event and claims I was the reason why we did not perform well at trial. Now that's a chump attorney.

So where did this leave us? The defense attorney was quick to suggest to Judge DiFiglia that a directed verdict was in order. A directed verdict means the case couldn't possibly go to the jury to ask them to render a decision because there simply and obviously wasn't any (or sufficient) evidence to need to involve the jury to decide the case, and the judge could dismiss my case entirely like it was totally frivolous and without merit or grounds. Why do you think the judge claimed this was a miscarriage of justice?

You could say I had totally lost my faith in Mr. Quinn to adequately represent our case by the third day in the trial. So then Judge DiFiglia told the two attorneys to go home and figure out a way out of this. They did, and it didn't end up being very pretty, either.

At the beginning of the fourth and last day of trial, the defense attorney said before we were to continue our trial, he'd like to discuss settling the case with us. Mr. Quinn recommended we listen to the proposal.

They offered us $3,000 in cash and another share certificate in the same company that Mr. Quinn had announced to the jury that the last couple of quarters of revenue were zero . . . to go away. With the way the trial had progressed, Mr. Quinn recommended we take this settlement and walk. That's right. At this point, I had lost so many hundreds of thousands of dollars and they wanted me to be happy with $3,000 and a certificate for more shares in the same fraudulent company.

The defendants also told us they were wrapping up a $2 million dollar cash infusion deal with a "White Knight," an undisclosed Texas investor, which would jumpstart the company again and the share certificate would certainly make us whole. Besides, the lone defendant who did not show up for trial was in default and we could proceed to collect from him also. Mr. Quinn instructed me to tell Judge DiFiglia the terms of the settlement were acceptable to me and I was to tell the judge just one word when asked if the settlement was acceptable—yes. After this travesty, $3,000 was better than nothing.

Then there developed another slight problem. Several weeks after this matter transpired, I realized Mr. Quinn only had to audibly inform the judge in front of the court recorder at the trial about the details of the settlement discussions we had with the defendants and the defense attorney. This all would have been recorded by the court recorder at the time, and would have been properly documented. However, at the trial and after having verbal discussions with the defense attorney and the defendants about how to settle our entire claim, Mr. Quinn failed to accurately and properly document what was said regarding the "White Knight" or as attorneys call it, "commence the terms of these settlement discussions" on record, then argued with the defense attorney about it a month later via e-mails, and made the mistake of sharing the following e-mails with me.

On October 30, 2002, 11:47 a.m., Mr. Kaeder sent an e-mail to Mr. Quinn:

Mr. Kaeder: "The document you sent was totally unsatisfactory because it attempted to hold the individuals accountable for ABC's performance and contained warranties that were never part of the deal."

On October 30, 2002, 12:46 p.m., with "High" importance, Mr. Quinn sent an e-mail back to Mr. Kaeder:

Mr. Quinn: My client "relied upon the representation about the $2 million Texas 'white knight' in agreeing to settle for the shares and a small amount of cash. This representation was a material inducement to settling. It must be listed in the settlement agreement as a representation that was made and relied upon."

On October 31, 2002, 11:10 a.m., Mr. Kaeder sent an e-mail to Mr. Quinn:

Mr. Kaeder: "Darren, The terms of the settlement are on the record. Under no circumstances was talk about another investment part of the agreement. Further, I would never have allowed it. I have the $3,000 in trust. You have not told me how to make out the share certificate. Since you haven't responded, it will be made out to all the plaintiffs. If you try to enforce anything else, I will request sanctions."

On October 31, 2002, 11:27 a.m. with "High" importance, Mr. Quinn sent an e-mail to Mr. Kaeder:

Mr. Quinn: "Your clients made certain representations that induced my clients to enter into the settlement (e.g., $2 million Texas investor) in ABC. Your integration clause language nullifies those representations."

On November 01, 2002, 12:38 p.m. Mr. Kaeder sends an email to Mr. Quinn:

Mr. Kaeder: "Darren, This is the last time. REMOVE THE WHEREAS ABOUT THE WHITE KNIGHT. That was not part of the settlement. You are trying to set my clients up for another lawsuit. Don't tell me about conditions, covenants, etc. I will not permit my clients to sign that document as is under any circumstances.

Please advise me in writing if you are going to try to force the issue. I want to see a transcript of the settlement on the record. Stop wasting my time. If you persist, I will ask for sanctions. Let me know what you are going to do at the ex parte on Tuesday. I DEMAND TO SEE YOUR PAPERS ASAP. I demand to know if you are going to tell the judge this White Knight bullshit is part of the deal. If you are, I'm going to show up to oppose and you will be paying the bill."

Somebody was lying here. One of these two so-called judicial professionals was lying. Take your pick as to which one it was. I think it's obvious Mr. Quinn couldn't do his job for multiple reasons and I believe he was scared. He was indeed most likely going to be sanctioned or fined by the courts for his incompetent stunt if he pushed Mr. Kaeder any futher on this issue.

You see, when Mr. Quinn stood before the judge after the settlement discussions, Mr. Quinn simply did not mention the discussion of the $2 million dollar investment that would reignite the ABC company and make the settlement a credible deal. Just so you know, I think I know why Mr. Quinn did this. I believe he and Mr. Kaeder crafted this little stunt purposefully and did this to avoid an immediate malpractice lawsuit by me against Mr. Quinn. This masterful plan would allow both of them off the hook. This might be hard for some folks to understand, but attorneys have a way of weaseling out of bad situations to save their own bacon . . . at the ultimate sacrifice of the client. I also believe Mr. Quinn was scared that Judge DiFiglia would take Mr. Kaeder's side and because Judge DiFiglia already had about enough of Mr. Quinn's circus stunts and incompetence in this case. Mr. Quinn settled the case at trial and failed to put the details on the record. Now you can see Mr. Quinn has boxed himself into yet another corner that he can't get out of it without me being the victim again.

(So you understand, if the $2 million dollars does not come into the company from the "White Knight" investor, the company is worthless and so are the settlement shares. Thus, Mr. Quinn's recommended settlement becomes a really bad recommendation on his part.)

So, can you guess what Mr. Quinn did? Do you think the terms were on the settlement record? Did Mr. Quinn do his job?

When a person assists a criminal in breaking the law before the criminal gets arrested, we call him an accomplice.

When a person assists a criminal in breaking the law after the criminal gets arrested, we call him a defense lawyer.

For the record, Mr. Quinn gave up and never did his job as you would expect an attorney to do, such as clearly listing the settlement discussions in detail, which accurately described what the fraudulent charged defendants said they would do and agreed to do if I settled with them. In addition to coughing up $3,000 and a new 1,250,000-share certificate, they agreed to wrap up the $2 million cash infusion deal with the "White Knight" investor to jumpstart the company. You see, if Mr. Quinn didn't record the details stating that the defendants had to make good on their statements that the company would get in gear and do more business, etc., then the whole idea of settling the case was worthless.

Also, Mr. Quinn was off the hook for his shenanigan of sandbagging the evidence, unlawfully obtaining the bank accounts of the "dirtiest defendant," and not presenting our evidence to the jury as he should have.

Worst of all, the three defendants who actually took the money in the company and spent it all—that is Joe Lindquist, Tom Carter, and John Cole—were dismissed from the case. In addition—and the most disgusting revelation on attorney incompetence—Mr. Quinn either forgot or intentionally dismissed the previously established "defaulted" ABC company, which I should have gotten a judgment against. They all were scott-free! And Mr. Quinn expects to bill for this?

And what of the $3,000 settlement check?

It wasn't made out to me; Mr. Kaeder made it out from his office to Mr. Darren J. Quinn, my attorney.

Do you suppose Mr. Quinn sent me a check for $3,000?

No.

Did Mr. Quinn retain this money for his own benefit and apply it to his bill?

Yes.

Where do you suppose the share certificate was sent?

Yes, to Mr. Quinn.

Did he retain the certificate in his possession?

Yes.

For how long do you suppose he retained this certificate?

A couple of days, maybe? Would you believe a couple of years?

Did Mr. Quinn apply the value of the shares to his bill like he did with the $3,000? Did Mr. Quinn apply one penny's worth of the certificate to his bill?

No.

Why did Mr. Quinn do this?

Mr. Quinn had racked up well over $40,000 of new legal fees in this process, and kept the share certificate from me since he considered it his, as he had a lien on my recovery. This is what attorneys will do if their bills are not paid in full . . . they want your assets.

In my own signed agreement with Mr. Quinn, it clearly stated that if his fee balance went over $5,000, that Mr. Quinn and I had an agreement on how this balance would be addressed. Sure enough, Mr. Quinn ran up the bill and exercised his lien on any recovery money he obtained as a result of him handling my case.

Mr. Quinn continued this whole settlement crap and dragged me into another appeal process that lasted for years, meanwhile still claiming I was entitled to $2.7 million dollars in damages from the "no show" fourth defendant— Timothy J. Connor—who did not show up to trial to defend himself.

Did I sue Mr. Quinn for this? I really couldn't justifiably yet because finally in November of 2003, Mr. Quinn obtained a judgment against Tim Connor and I needed to see if I could collect from him. As the laws of the land allow, Mr. Connor appealed the judgment, plus Mr. Quinn wanted more action!

In light of the outcome of the trial, the settlement was supposed to be such a good one. Mr. Quinn argued since the fraud was so bad, I was entitled to $2.7 million dollars in damages . . . this is above the actual or compensatory damages. And this was no problem, because we were free to go after these damages against the lone-star defendant who didn't show up for trial. This was the master plan. But there became yet another problem (one of many, actually).

I asked Mr. Quinn to secure an asset freeze on this lone-star defendant's assets to secure our interests. Mr. Quinn never did, even after repeated attempts of me asking him to do this and then demanding him to do it.

In the end of the appeal process in January of 2006, Mr. Quinn got a confirmation of the $660,000 judgment against the lone-star defendant, Tim Connor. (There was no mention of what happened to the $2.7 million dollar claim.)

This is a piece of paper signed by the judge that says the defendant is ordered to pay me this much money . . . this is not a check from the judicial system to me. It's just a piece of paper. That sounds better than nothing, until I tell you that during 2006, I had to hire another attorney to attempt to collect on this judgment. Mr. Quinn wouldn't do anything with the judgment piece of paper. He just said he didn't do collections! I never received one penny from this judgment.

Mr. Tim Connor filed for bankruptcy and stopped the collection efforts in the process. By the time this appeal/bankruptcy process was all over, Mr. Connor and his assets were nowhere to be found. He disappeared along with his assets. Mr. Connor escaped the law, my civil judgment, and never paid me one penny.

Remember how the company was defaulted at trial? It shouldn't come to any surprise that Mr. Quinn's failed handling of my case to obtain a separate judgment against the company also left me with an empty judicial bag of restitution, and no way to collect from the company, either. Remember all the charges were dismissed. Mr. Quinn didn't do one thing with the defaulted status of the ABC company.

Mr. Quinn's favorable result, even though its basis "didn't pass the lawyer smell test," which you will later learn about, consisted of three identifiable results:

1. $3,000 that he directly deposited for himself;

2. A share certificate of 1,250,000 shares for the same company we sued and Mr. Quinn retained these shares until they were of no real value (covered in further detail later);

3. An uncollectable judgment over $660,000 against the defaulted defendant who was merely an accomplice who was paid around $30,000 commission on the fraudulent transaction! Again, this judgment was later determined to be uncollectable and totally worthless because I was never paid one penny of this judgment against Tim Connor.

Then Mr. Quinn released the company and the other three defendants from the lawsuit—the ones who took the money! Mr. Connor remains at large today while the total judgement value against Mr. Connor is well over $1 million dollars with added interest. I most likely will never, ever see one penny of this civil judgment.

God decided to take the devil to court and settle their differences once and for all. When Satan heard this, he laughed and said, "And where do you think you're going to find a lawyer?"

After seven years and all this time, money, and effort I was disheartened and upset to learn I wouldn't collect a dime. And after extensive and expensive efforts to attempt to collect on the judgment, I conceded after three recommendations, to file fraud charges against attorney Darren J. Quinn. I really didn't want to, but when you exhaust every avenue your attorney has guided you through and you end up with an empty jar, can you blame me?

I was out of options and utterly disgusted. I was down to the last straw. It was time to sue the attorney for the losses since I surely felt he had not done even a substandard job of being a lawyer. I followed his recommendations and paid his fee balances right up until just a few months before the trial and I witnessed the result of his services and fees. I decided then he had ulterior motives.

I refrained from filing a malpractice suit immediately after trial because I still wanted to give him every chance to make it right but the findings and results only continued down the same pathway. It was the last chance for restitution in the grand scheme of things.

I realize in most walks of life, people are going to make mistakes. But in most of these walks of life occupations, the people are kind of expected to correct those mistakes . . . one way or another. In industry, if we made mistakes, they were quickly and immediately addressed and corrected. Otherwise the public and the media would be all over it. If a commercial pilot makes a mistake, the result is clearly and immediately noticed by the absence or presence of a safe landing at the intended destination's airport.

This is one thing that pisses off most Americans when it comes to attorneys—they think their performance doesn't matter. Attorneys think they are entitled to get paid outrageous rates even when they screw up this badly.

Meanwhile, I was running out of straws. I had lost so much money and had only piled on the losses with getting Mr. Quinn involved. I had witnessed the pathetic fact of my case evidence lost in a hoodwinking haze of a hocus-pocus flimflam sham. This just was more than I could accept . . . defeat when I knew I was in the right and had been grossly wronged.

After carefully reviewing the result Mr. Quinn generated and carefully considering my only remaining options to seek and search for justice, the last straw was to sue Mr. Quinn for malpractice, which I never dreamed would ever need to happen.

I searched for a legal representative to set this concept into motion. It's not hard to find attorneys who will sue other attorneys who commit fraud . . . if the stage is properly set. There are some attorneys who don't particularly care for rogue attorneys giving them all a bad name . . . believe it or not. Of course, the vast majority isn't keen on the idea of suing a fraternity brother, but if they can make hordes of money, then I believe you generally can count them in.

I found out from talking to a few that if you mention up front how much money you lost, that will perk them up and get their attention and interest. That's because they think they'll get a nice fat percentage of it!

Once I realized the civil courts would not and could not provide the justice that was in order, I fully endorsed the idea in my mind that Mr. Quinn should indeed pay for such a despicable performance of his actions . . . especially when he thought he should be paid in full regarding his bills, in light of his outlandish performance and stunts.

I found another attorney and he reviewed my situation. He quickly assessed the performance of Mr. Quinn's actions of the lack of professional conduct and filed a malpractice lawsuit against Mr. Quinn in the California state courts. To yet another eye opening result, I was denied a legal jury trial and later ordered by the California state court to resolve the case in what is called Arbitration with a so-called arbitrator. This arbitrator would decide the case.

An attorney or legal counsel is not required in this process, and the attorney who filed my case against Mr. Quinn simply told me he could not in good conscience charge me to represent me in this process because he knew I had been severely misrepresented by the system and already suffered enough loss. Besides, he told me I certainly could present my case well enough on my own and that the facts would speak for themselves. I most assuredly agreed.

An arbitrator for this non-trial/jury process is supposed to be a neutral referee or umpire type of person who is to serve as an impartial party to resolve and settle a dispute between two parties that can't come to agreeable terms. In a more, let's call it a mutually acceptable setting, arbitration is an agreed upon forum to settle disputes between parties in lieu of going to a full-blown litigation lawsuit.

Except in my case, when it comes to attorneys, the whole arbitration process was mandated against my will and rights, as I demanded a jury trial—a panel of ordinary citizens.

The attorney who filed the fraud case against Mr. Quinn even argued my right to a jury trial and lost in front of the presiding judge. This was very upsetting to this attorney and to me, too. We both wanted a jury trial; we wanted a jury to see just what Mr. Quinn did; and we wanted a jury of ordinary citizens to decide what should be the resolution of my mess.

Looking back, it would have been nice to have Mr. Quinn just file a motion for summary judgment when the defendants had not answered the questions back in October of 2001. Could this whole mess of injustice have been avoided? I think so.

How can you tell when a lawyer is lying?

His lips are moving.

CHAPTER 3:

THE ROOT OF IT ALL

OUR SOCIETY HAS CHANGED. Maybe it's just me but I have a hard time understanding the newer and more modern-day liberal ways compared to the old-fashioned country upbringing I received. In my mind, things were different back then. For one, lying carried a penalty. I'd like to think that it wasn't all that long ago either.

Unlike today, if you were caught lying as a child and depending on the infraction, you might expect to receive a paddling. Yes, a paddling. These days, that will get you thrown in jail. You just can't do it. But you sure can lie and get by with it though, can't you?

I believe that our society has become just a little complacent with respect to being respectful of others. Respect requires some integrity. And to have integrity you need to have a basic underlying set of principles that should include honesty. I fear we are becoming a nation based on telling people what they want to hear rather than telling it like it is.

When is the last time you ever heard of a politician being labeled as a "straight shooter," a "tell it like it is," or "give 'em hell Harry" kind of person? Growing up back in the 1960s and 1970s, maybe I was just too secluded from the modern-day societies of the big cities, but I just don't recall people of good sound principles and character being called, "whistle blowers" if they reported actual facts as they are. How many times do you see on *60 Minutes, Dateline,* or NPT about a story where someone was a whistle blower and lost his or her job as a result? Nowadays, we single them out like they are actual convicts. How has our society evolved to this?

We have bred generations of people who believe lying is acceptable and is an ordinary part of life as we lead it. To this extent, I also believe we, as a nation, have turned our morals equally away from pride and integrity, and I feel that attorneys have cast their lying hypocritical ways upon society in an even bigger way—into our democratic government system, too.

I am concerned that Americans are blind-folded and sheepish as to what is occurring on the local and national stages with justice, and it's these demented hypocritical methodologies that have for too long been integrated into politics. Telling the truth versus telling the public what they want to hear has become the standard in politics. Politicians aren't interested in what's going on in the public sector of this country. The majority of them have been solely in it for the money. Why else would the concept of campaign contributions even exist?

We only need to look at history to see the uncanny similarities between our present society and one just 200 years ago.

Alexander Fraser Tytler, Lord Woodhouselee (1747–1813) was a lawyer, writer, historian, and professor. Tytler spoke of how societies erode by means of corruption and bribery within government, and how disinterested people submit to the abandonment of their natural liberties as if they were under a monarchy. He also generalized that the spirit and love of ingenious freedom eventually exit from great nations. As history repeats itself, there are no irregularities where wealth is diminished by the decay of once valiant morals and ethics.

This is where we are today and we all know that history repeats itself, don't we?

The sad part about this is that most Americans won't act upon this sickening, moldy plague until it affects them directly. Sadly, it has already affected quite a significant number. Odds are good that either you, someone in your family, or someone you know has had a less-than-upstanding result from a legal case due to greed, unethical actions, a technicality, or plain laziness.

Isn't it amazing how attorneys don't want results of their court cases listed somewhere for public viewing? Conversely, the public sure wants to know how many recalls an automobile manufacturer or a food processor has if it directly affects them.

• • •

When I was in high school, one of my favorite classes was Biology, largely because the teacher had taught the class for many years and had the teaching part down very well. His name was Mr. Stephens. Mr. Stephens had a favorite saying: "Easy disease, there's a fungus among us." I would contend we indeed have a fungus among us in America today.

To give you some further perspective on this hint, before I started attempting to put my evidence together on my fraud case against Mr. Quinn, I was shocked to discover a basic principle regarding case law: the judicial system assumes you are lying and you have to prove you're not. I could not believe what I read. These days, the justice system believes both parties are assumed to give untruthful testimonies and the system has the task to determine which party is telling more of the truth as it relates to what actually happened. When I read that I just about flipped out of my chair. Instead of "being innocent until proven guilty," why don't they just say it like it is: You're guilty until proven innocent, regardless of whether you are a plaintiff or a defendant.

None of this affected anything I was setting out to do though, because my case wasn't based on "hearsay" or solely what some witness saw or heard. My case was based on what I put together from actual documented events, which were by trial transcripts, documents, e-mails, and letters. That's exactly what I told the arbitrator during my first preliminary hearing when he asked how many witnesses I was going to have. I told him very few because this case was on paper and pretty much in black and white. So, I wasn't worried about having to be judged as to whether or not I was lying. In fact, I was looking forward to getting my evidence aired.

There was no way I could have known I was going to be slaughtered in attempting this process. In fact, the Arbitrator even told me during the first preliminary hearing on October 18, 2007, weeks before the fullblown Arbitration hearing, I was entitled to "Due Process of Law" by using the arbitration process. Boy, did this ever end up being the farthest from the truth.

I can't really give you a good definition or explanation of "Due Process of Law," based on my experience. I thought it was supposed to mean you were entitled to a fair and unbiased judicial chance at having a fair trial if you feel you were screwed in this country. But I can't say that is the case. That's not what due process means to me in this country. To me, it's a joke. Being quite frank about it, it means you have the opportunity to meet, first hand, Mr. Ben Dover and C. Howlett Fields, members of the Dewey, Cheatum, and Howe Law firm. You can most likely find one of these firms in your local neighborhood. The name might be slightly different to disguise the actual intent, but their purposes are about the same.

• • •

H. W. Prentis, president of the Armstrong Cork Company, gave a speech in 1943 called "Industrial Management in a Republic" and cited Alexander Fraser Tytler who was a Senator of the College of Justice and a renowned Professor in the following:

> The average age of the world's greatest civilizations from the beginning of history has been about two hundred years. During those two hundred years, these nations always progressed through the following pattern called "The Fatal Sequence":
>
> - From bondage to spiritual faith;
> - From spiritual faith to great courage;
> - From courage to liberty;
> - From liberty to abundance;
> - From abundance to selfishness;
> - From selfishness to complacency;
> - From complacency to apathy;
> - From apathy to dependence;
> - From dependence back into bondage.

At the stage between apathy and dependency, men always turn in fear to economic and political panaceas. New conditions, it is claimed, require new remedies. Under such circumstances, the competent citizen is certainly not a fool if he insists upon using the compass of history when forced to sail uncharted seas. Usually so-called new remedies are not new at all. Compulsory planned economy, for example, was tried by the Chinese some three millenniums ago, and by the Romans in the early centuries of the Christian era. It was applied in Germany, Italy and Russia long before the present war broke out. Yet it is being seriously advocated today as a solution of our economic problems in the United States. Its proponents confidently assert that government can successfully plan and control all major business activity in the nation, and still not interfere with our political freedom and our hard-won civil and religious liberties. The lessons of history all point in exactly the reverse direction."[1]

• • •

The rise and fall of the Roman Empire sequel here in America is nearing yet another completed "Fatal Sequence" cycle before our very eyes! Tytler, again in 1790, made this profound observation: "A democracy cannot exist as a permanent form of government. It can only exist until the majority discovers it can vote itself largess out of the public treasury."[2]

In the end, the majority always votes for the candidate promising the most benefits with the result insuring the democracy collapses because of the loose fiscal policy ensuing, always to be followed by a dictatorship, then a monarchy.

---

1 Henning Webb Prentis, Jr., "Industrial Management in a Republic," March 18, 1943, http://theconservativenation.com/2009/12/09/industrial-management-in-a-republic/.
2 Ibid.

If any one of you wants to exploit one of my greatest weaknesses, exploit this: the idea that I might have a phobia, where my personal case involves both dislike and fear. The fact is I dislike what the corrupt attorneys are doing to our society while the good ones watch, laugh, and let it happen; meanwhile I fear I seem to be the only concerned American to put on the table one of the leading causes of our modern-day "Fatal Sequence" reasons why we are in such a hellacious financial crisis in our history. Absolutely no one in the media is talking about the decay of our once heroic virtues that catapulted this infant nation to elite greatness. We have missed this vital contribution of fundamental reasons as to why our heroic virtues have vanished from prominence. Come on, Americans! Wake up for cryin' out loud! Alexander Fraser Tytler felt the exact same way and I believe we ought to take heed to his wisdom.

I'd like to think that in our modern society with all our competence, intelligence, brilliance, and arrogance, we could at least recognize the accuracy of previous historians like Tytler who obviously had an absurdly precise crystal ball.

We need our judicial system to police mankind's obvious appetite for greed—for the good of a freedom-loving nation—not demonstrate the judicial department's weakness and failure to succumb to the epitome of corruption!

Now for another piece of missing American history attorneys, lawyers, judges, politicians, and the media won't care for you to know about—the missing original 13th Amendment to the Constitution of the United States. What is this? In my opinion, it's the sole reason our republic is failing. Attorneys think they want to have ultimate power in not just the judicial branch of government, but the legislative and executive branch as well. Now that they've done it, is everyone satisfied with the consequential results?

CONTEMPT IN COURT

A small-town prosecuting attorney called his first witness to the stand in a trial—a grandmotherly, elderly woman. He approached her and asked, "Mrs. Jones, do you know me?"

She responded, "Why, yes, I do know you, Mr. Williams. I've known you since you were a young boy. And frankly, you've been a big disappointment to me. You lie, you cheat on your wife, you manipulate people and talk about them behind their backs. You think you're a rising big shot when you haven't the brains to realize you never will amount to anything more than a two-bit paper pusher. Yes, I know you."

The lawyer was stunned. Not knowing what else to do he pointed across the room and asked, "Mrs. Williams, do you know the defense attorney?"

She again replied, "Why, yes I do. I've known Mr. Bradley since he was a youngster, too. I used to baby-sit him for his parents. And he, too, has been a real disappointment to me. He's lazy, bigoted, and he has a drinking problem. The man can't build a normal relationship with anyone and his law practice is one of the shoddiest in the entire state. Yes, I know him."

At this point, the judge rapped the courtroom to silence and called both counselors to the bench. In a very quiet voice, he said with menace, "If either of you asks her if she knows me, you'll be in jail for contempt within five minutes!"

CHAPTER 4:

HIDE AND GO SEEK WITH EVIDENCE

DURING THE PREPARATION process for an Arbitration hearing with this attorney, there are a couple of worthwhile incidents that occurred. Witnessing what I call the "legal" art of an attorney playing his role is something you may even find amusing. I sure did. But before I roll into the meat and potatoes of the hearing, I'd like to provide you with an appetizer of a fairly detailed overview of a small procedural matter that may shed some light as to how attorneys can conduct themselves and might be considered above the law. And we'll see what you think.

Once I had filed a lawsuit against Mr. Quinn, he was apparently not allowed to legally represent himself so he had an attorney represent him who had a working relationship with him in his own office. His name was Paul M. DeCicco. I believe Mr. DeCicco was quite the classic defense attorney. He seemed to love to write condescending memos and dig at me in any way he could.

Mr. DeCicco would send e-mails that would include statements like:

> Your case is frivolous and brought for an improper purpose and by your childlike stonewalling you are admitting just that. You can't just file a case because you feel like it, because you are unhappy with the result of a prior proceeding, need to vent or want to get out of paying Mr. Quinn's bill . . . There are consequences for filing a suit without any good faith legal basis to do so and you are well advised to either withdraw your claims now or disclose the legal basis for maintaining your counter-claim when from all that we have reviewed, there is no *LEGAL* basis for maintaining an action against Mr. Quinn, no matter what spin is put on the facts.

In this incident, we were to exchange documents in our possession and control so the opposing party can see what evidence you have to build for your case and vice versa. I just loved the hide-and-go-seek game these attorneys played with me, and to think the system of justice depends on this process alone. Each party was to supply their documents to an independent source location called a "repository" for viewing the documents which was to be mutually accessible by both parties. Looking back, I recall getting the early picture I was going against a house of stacked cards.

Mr. DeCicco urged the Arbitrator to select his suggested source in San Diego. I had done a Map Quest and found this location was 17.39 miles from Mr. Quinn's and Mr. DeCicco's office and 2,052.1 miles from my house. So I sent a separate communication e-mail to note this disparity to the arbitration case manager and requested that an alternative equidistant source be chosen and stated I cannot travel over 2,000 miles to review their documents and evidence on any reasonable basis or cost. So I requested they ask Mr. Quinn and Mr. DeCicco to copy their evidence and forward it to me as I had already forwarded mine to literally their own back yard. I stated, this would be a "simple and realistic remedy" to this gross physical hindrance they put me in.

On October 29, 2007, the Arbitrator issued a "CLARIFYING RULING ON PARTY DOCUMENTS PRODUCTION" which refused to change this location and simply ordered each opposing party to have their evidence documents at the San Diego location by November 2, 2007, obviously ignoring the fact that I was over 2,000 miles away from this location. The order stated:

> The purpose of establishing said repository is to provide a neutral location whereby each party may deposit its relevant documentation for inspection by the opposing party. Each party shall solely assume the labor and costs associated with the transportation and placement of its relevant documentation into the repository, as herein ordered.

This order was an example and a clear sign of what fairness and impartiality was to come.

Now as a matter of just plain humor with regard to how Mr. Quinn's attorney, Mr. DiCicco acted as a professional attorney, here is part of an e-mail he wrote to me and copied the Arbitrator on November 7, 2007, regarding the very subject of document production:

> Mr. Quinn has had the opportunity to note the documents that you have deposited with Paulson Court Reporting. With regard thereto, there is only a handful of paper documents and some CD ROMS. My understanding from listening to you at the Preliminary Hearings and knowing what was turned over to you by Mr. Quinn prior to the instant arbitration, was that there were at least ten banker's boxes of relevant original documents in your possession and control. The bulk of such documents comprises the original file that you

requested from Mr. Quinn sometime ago. I understand that some of these documents may have been produced in CD ROM form and many appear at first blush to be represented by electronic duplicates on the CD ROMs now on deposit. However, the CD ROMs that were reviewed did not include any indication of two of the sequentially referenced original boxes of documents. In other words, there seem to be two (or more) boxes of documents that are still NOT on deposit at Paulson, in any form. Could you please follow-up and let me know the status of the apparently missing boxes of documents?

Additionally, it was my understanding that you would be depositing the original paper documents that comprised Mr. Quinn's file. Without our being able to review the original documents it is impossible to determine if you have produced the universe of documents that your [yes, this is correctly quoted misspelled] were required to produce by the order of the Arbitrator. Indeed it appears that you have NOT since as the set of CD-ROMs at the depository. Claimant Quinn has produced all of his documents on CD ROM, because that is the way that were kept in the ordinary course of business. There are no relevant paper documents in Claimant's possession or control, that I am aware of.

Mr. DeCicco goes on to state,

You appear to be motivated to continue with your counter-claim by pure unbridled emotion which has perversely manifested in an irrational and malicious intent towards Mr. Quinn and has blinded you to reason . . . You admit that you agree with my assessment that your suit is without merit, and is being continued purely out of malice, ill will and a desire to vex Mr. Quinn . . . You continue to posture as if you have valid claims, simply to vex Mr. Quinn, perhaps in an attempt to get him to compromise the amount of money that you owe him and/or simply because you, for some twisted reason known only to, wish him ill will.

Not many people I know in the industry or in the piloting world use the word "vex" so I'd like to provide the *Webster's Dictionary* definition:

> **Vex:** *1. To annoy by petty irritations. 2. To trouble or afflict.*
> *3. To baffle, puzzle, or confuse.*

Did you catch a few little innuendoes within this excerpt from Mr. DeCicco?

First, they originally had all the files, copied them, gave them to me, and now "it is impossible for them to determine if I had produced the universe of documents." They also claim some boxes seem to be missing and I am supposed to know where they are.

Apparently it's also OK that I have to go through all of Quinn's CD ROM files, 2,052.1 miles away, but it is impossible for them to go through the CDs of the entire files already in their possession. They need the originals. How does this disparity exist and for what purpose, do you suppose?

So, does Mr. DeCicco's lack of awareness of "no relevant" documents in Mr. Quinn's possession or control constitute justification in his own mind that he has no further legal responsibility to produce and place everything in the repository as by the order of the Arbitrator? In other words, does Mr. DeCicco think that he doesn't have to give me access to their documents because he doesn't think I can make a case against Mr. Quinn without them?

And how could my actions of filing a basic lawsuit for alleging fraud, malpractice, conversion, deceit, etc., possibly bring any such vexing, and possibly cause ill will to an attorney who does this thing as ordinary daily business to other people? Besides, how could a lay person, by attorneys' standards, possibly bring forth a matter against an attorney "by pure unbridled emotion" unless there was some slight possibility—an inkling of truth and some evidence of Mr. Quinn's actions and some tracks that were left—that just possibly might cause him to lose his license to practice law?

If there was no harm or foul play whatsoever on behalf of Mr. Quinn, why didn't they just turn over my files with no hassle immediately in the beginning? Maybe they didn't take as much time as they thought they should have going over the files before they turned them over to me, and now that the stakes were more serious than they previously could have thought, they wanted the originals brought back to their coveted repository where they could pour through the entire "universe" of documents and cull any discriminating evidence that could possibly be damaging to Mr. Quinn's case and his livelihood.

I personally believe Mr. DeCicco was missing the point of me filing a lawsuit against Mr. Quinn if his well-chosen word "vex" was appropriately used in his context. Filing a lawsuit for fraud certainly wasn't just to irritate him or confuse him. If that were the case, I could have written a letter to the editor of his local newspaper describing his performance and it wouldn't have cost me a dime. That being said, you might well surmise that if you file a lawsuit for anything in your life, according to the world Mr. DeCicco lives in, you're likely just wanting to irritate your defendant and confuse them, and your attorney is just helping and assisting you provide that irritation, not that you will expect a real result or anything else like restitution or making a matter right or getting your money back. Again, lawsuits are all about providing irritation.

These are the same two attorneys who responded back on January 4, 2007, to my request to receive all my files and documents of my entire case and this is what Mr. Quinn prepared for me to pick up at his office when I flew 2,000 miles to San Diego to pick the documents up.

I had expected to pick up over ten bankers boxes of our case files and this was it. I was so moved by Mr. Quinn's inaction to completely fulfill my request for my entire files that I took this one and only little box with its contents back to my hotel room and took this picture. This picture is exactly what Mr. Quinn prepared for me to pick up. This box contained the total case files that Mr. Quinn had generated from 1999 to 2006 through all this litigation and that I paid tens of thousands of dollars for. The writing on the box is exactly as I picked it up.

Can you guess why Mr. Quinn prepared only this little box of documents for me to pick up? Do you suppose it was because by this time he knew and anticipated the likelihood for my filing a malpractice and fraud lawsuit against him and he wasn't about to turn over crucifying evidence without first being able to go through it and ditch or dispose of or pull evidence that he did not want used against him. That's a thought.

Hear about the terrorist that hijacked a 747 full of lawyers?

He threatened to release one every hour if his demands weren't met.

Now you can see the difference in how attorneys can toy with evidence. I'd prefer to call it tampering with the evidence, especially when it comes to lawsuits that are targeting themselves. Who knows better than attorneys as to how evidence can be used, and especially when it can possibly be used against them?

I finally had to file a formal complaint with the California State Bar about Mr. Quinn not returning my files to me. My formal complaint cited the California law governing attorneys and your rights to your own files in the attorney's possession. That law is Rule 3-700D, which I've taken from the California Legal Ethics Library:

> Both MR 1.16 and CRPC 3-700 require a lawyer to return all of the client's papers and property to the client upon termination of representation and require the return of the unearned part of any fee advance.

It worked, but only to a point of devious reply.

Mr. Quinn informed me that my files were now located at a copy/scan shop in San Diego and they could be picked up there. So I contacted them and they wanted 15 cents per page or $390 for each box and there were more than ten of them.

The person I spoke with said he was a good friend of Mr. Quinn and had known him for years. Now that's a bias, buddy. They wanted to charge me for my files. So, I had to send another letter to the California State Bar explaining that Mr. Quinn and his friend at the copy/scan shop wanted over $4,000 from me before I could pick up my files. (Do you suppose Mr. Quinn, as an attorney, really just didn't know this violated ethics rules and do you suppose he just thought this might just be another way to milk another $4,000 or more out of the client just one last time?)

It wasn't long until I received another letter from Mr. Quinn stating, "I have authorized CopyScan to release the documents to you without the necessity of you first copying your files at your cost." And Mr. Quinn also stated in the same letter, "I am disappointed that you complained to the State Bar rather than communicate with me directly."

As his client, I went to the trouble to communicate directly with him on January 4, 2007, and you saw the box picture of documents he had prepared for me, so what would you do? On February 13, 2006, nearly one full year earlier, Mr. Quinn sent me his formal notice letter that he had concluded his services and the lustrous laws of the land provide a one-year statute of limitation time frame to bring a lawsuit against an attorney, so my time was quickly running out and I had not yet filed an action against Mr. Quinn, although one thing was for sure: He knew I was far from happy with his legal representation. That's why I needed to summons help from the State Bar to get my files out of his possession before he was formally served with a fraud lawsuit. Mr. Quinn was likely suspecting this anyway but the deadline was fast approaching.

It took until March 16, 2007, before my files were available for me to pick them up! What do you suppose Mr. Quinn and Mr. DeCicco did with those files between January 4, 2007, and March 16, 2007? I'm sure they sat there untouched just waiting to be picked up, don't you think? But then again, how did the entire file of my documents for a trial case in the previous picture grow from the one little box to the 9 or 10 or more bankers boxes of documents that you previously read about from the quoted words from Mr. DeCicco? Is this a mystery? No, it's really what happened.

And for clarification, this whole arbitration file issue transpired after Mr. Quinn and Mr. DeCicco had copied my files and already had the copied files in their possession. What a picture Mr. DeCicco painted to the Arbitrator that I was not cooperating with them to get them all the files they already had in their possession and copied, but it sure made them look like they were struggling with me to get the files they righteously needed and were entitled to.

One thing is for sure, I'll never know what documents were missing from my files and how much time Mr. Quinn and Mr. DeCicco spent pouring over each and every file from January 4, 2007, until March 16, 2007. But it sure seemed to be a sensitive issue for them for some reason as from Mr. DeCicco's quoted words and the abundance of effort to thwart turning over my files until the State Bar moved the process forward.

At a convention of biological scientists one researcher remarked to another, "Did you know that in our lab we have switched from mice to lawyers for our experiments?"

"Really?" the other replied, "Why did you switch?"

"Well, for three reasons. First we found that lawyers are far more plentiful; second, the lab assistants don't get so attached to them; and thirdly there are some things even a rat won't do."

Is this how you would like to have your case handled and replied to by defense counsel if you were the Plaintiff? You can check with the California State Bar today and see for yourself if Mr. Quinn ever had a complaint filed against him for violating the ethics law regarding client files rights and guess what you will find—nothing! But try removing a speeding violation off your driving record and see where you get.

A REASONABLE FEE

A man phones a lawyer and asks, "How much would you charge for just answering three simple questions?"

The lawyer replies, "A thousand dollars."

"A thousand dollars!" exclaims the man. "That's very expensive isn't it?"

"It certainly is," says the lawyer. "Now, what's your third question?"

CHAPTER 5:

ARBITRATION TRIAL

IT WAS WEDNESDAY, December 5, 2007, in San Marcos, California, just north of San Diego at the University of Phoenix facility where the hearing had been scheduled to take place, and was I looking forward to airing my evidence against the attorney who had led me on an emotional roller coaster and down a path of financial destruction. The hearing was scheduled for two full days: Wednesday and Thursday per my request and the request of the opposing attorney. I was claiming fraud charges along with a whole host of other charges.

The hearing was scheduled to start at 9:30 a.m. I arrived right at 9:00 and went up to the second floor with all my briefcases and files and proceeded to the room reserved for us. The room was an ordinary classroom like in any school setting with the exception of having individual armchairs. There were several large round tables with chairs around each table. I was the first one there by no surprise, so I took advantage of the quiet time to get out my binders of evidence, notes, and questions and started doing a brief overview, when, in a few minutes, a young woman walked into the room pulling a case on wheels. She asked if this was the room for the arbitration and I confirmed it was. I asked what she was here for and she told me she was a court recorder. Her name was Sharon. I thought, how interesting. So I asked Sharon, "who hired you to be here today?"

She replied that Mr. DeCicco, the defense counsel for Mr. Quinn, had hired her. Well, this was an interesting development. Why would two attorneys hire a court recorder for an arbitration hearing? Could it be he might be fearful of losing and he might need to appeal the decision? If you were planning on a slam dunk, you wouldn't think you would need to go to the expense of hiring a court recorder to document everything that was said, would you? The court recorder was friendly and didn't have a dog in this fight so she freely conversed with me as she set up to perform her duties with her recording equipment.

As 9:30 approached, I started to wonder if anybody else was going to make it when the arbitrator walked in. We exchanged greetings and the arbitrator wanted to arrange some of the tables in the room for the hearing. He wanted to position himself at one table in the middle of the room next to the chalkboard and he wanted two other tables set to his front with one on each side of him. I assisted in locating the tables and had just finished with this when, in walks the defense, nearly fifteen minutes late and with an excuse. There was my former attorney, who I last saw when we were on speaking terms, on September 19, 2002, the last day of our dreadful trial.

It had been over five years since I had been face-to-face with him on a more freely and open basis, and let's say I was about as happy to see him as he was to see me. (After all, he was billed the same amount I was by the

Arbitration Association for that day's hearing: $10,500). He strolled in with his own attorney, Mr. DeCicco. I had listened to all his ranting leading up to today. Plus, one more individual accompanied them, who I shortly learned was yet another attorney.

I thought, *Well now, either somebody is extremely scared he is going to lose or this guy knows his own capability and he needs all the help he can get.* They were all three carrying as much as they could pack under each arm. Each one had their own laptop computer and they brought along their own big screen projector. (Take specific note of this because I'm going to bring this up again in greater detail). I marveled at all the props they came prepared with. It certainly looked like they were ready for battle. So, there I was, by myself, positioned at one round table, and there were three attorneys sitting at the other table to the right side of the arbitrator. The arbitrator instructed the court recorder to be located near the center of us all so she could clearly hear any one of us from her vantage point.

The showdown stage was set and that was the quietest I had ever seen my former attorney in all the years prior. He never spoke out loud, and sat between the other two attorneys only whispering to each of them. I might also mention that he didn't care to make long eye contact sessions with me either. He knew the charges against him and he knew what he did.

Furthermore, he had received a copy of my evidence against him that I had prepared for this hearing. I had to prepare four three-inch, three-ring binders each consisting of 74 tabbed sections and 283 pages of evidence. A copy was supplied to the Arbitrator, a copy to the defense attorney Mr. DeCicco, and one copy to Mr. Quinn himself weeks before this hearing date. So they had ample time to pour through my evidence against them and prepare their defense.

Maybe I was foolish putting myself in this predicament but I have been in the hot seat on many occasions in my career with my job. This type of stage was all too often the spot light in the automobile industry when you have millions of dollars worth of assembly line tooling and are about to launch a new car line and a new vehicle needs to roll off the assembly line every 25 seconds or someone is going to get charged $26,000 for each one lost. Failures weren't tolerated with complacency and latitude, like I've experienced with the system of justice. Maybe my tolerance for substandard results in my career was something new for Mr. Quinn. He knew full well I wasn't kidding around since I'd dragged him into quite a little predicament to where maybe he wasn't so sure of his fate. Besides, this wasn't an automotive business for some large corporation's benefit; this was my business involving my own money!

Lawyer's creed: A man is innocent until proven broke.

There were two previous telephone conference calls before this hearing. These phone calls were called preliminary meetings to lay down the rules and guidelines of the hearing. I clearly recall during the first one, the arbitrator asked Mr. Quinn if he was fully aware of the consequences of the charges against him if he was found guilty and the arbitrator made sure he was aware he could lose his license to practice law if he was found guilty of fraud.

Furthermore, the Arbitrator asked me if I was aware of what could happen to Mr. Quinn's livelihood and career as an attorney if he was found guilty and I told him I certainly was. Ironically, with insuring each party was fully aware of the possible consequences, Mr. Quinn never once attempted to or never once offered to reduce his bill to settle the dispute, and marched head on into this hearing. Looking back, it seems clearer, either he was missing more marbles than I had suspected, or he knew a whole lot more about the upcoming forum and process than any non-attorney person could have known.

Back to the first day of the hearing. As the hearing got underway, the Arbitrator met resistance to proceeding with the hearing itself! Yes, Mr. DeCicco started arguing with the Arbitrator making the accusation that I wasn't even entitled to have a hearing on the matter and that I couldn't prove anything because he had seen the evidence. He demanded a ruling on a statute time-barred motion he had submitted to the Arbitrator that should ban my right to the hearing. This went on for probably around 20 to 30 minutes.

Mr. DeCicco just didn't want to give up on the attempt to argue his point that Mr. Quinn's last work or action was over one calendar year ago and that his letter giving notice of his conclusion wasn't and shouldn't be considered as his final representation and the whole matter should be dismissed upon a matter of technicality. I sat there concerned, of course, about this possibly happening but then my sentiment turned to silent amusement when finally the bickering discussion between DeCicco and the Arbitrator stopped, and the Arbitrator overruled DeCicco's objection and stated, "What I want to make sure, though, is that at the end of this process, realizing this is an adversarial process and arbitration is very likely, that someone is not going to like the results." He went on to say, "As one of the new arbitrator trainers for American Arbitration Association for the last ten years, I'm very, very cognizant of what my authority is and the areas in which I have the zone of discretion."

The Arbitrator next proceeded to accept my counter claim against Mr. Quinn, which had accrued with interest to nearly $940,000. Even though Mr. DeCicco's rambling was a waste of time and money, it diminished the allotted time I had to put on my evidence.

The Arbitrator asked me to raise my right arm and asked, "Do you swear that the testimony you're about to give in this arbitration hearing shall be the truth, the whole truth, and nothing but the truth, so help you God?"

I answered, "I do." Then, he asked me to walk him through my evidence to support my claim. I stated, "I would like to call Darren J. Quinn as my first witness."

You should have seen the look on everybody's faces except the court recorder. If and only if I had a camera to show you just how beet red Mr. Quinn's face got for the next 45–60 seconds. If there were a thermometer attached to his face, it would have busted the glass by the mercury spike. Apparently it's not normal in litigation to call the defense as your first witness.

After our underlying case against the original defendants, Mr. Quinn told me afterwards that he had gone to a training seminar for attorneys and that it helps win cases if you call your key defense witness first and use them to enter much of the case evidence. This approach has many positive benefits as it puts them on the witness stand, taxes them in front of the judge for what seems like eternity, tires and wears them out just having to be on total alert for all the basic background of the case since they were involved and you get to hear what they are going to say regarding the truth or not . . . so you know what areas they lie about that you'll have to counter. You sort of pin them down as to what happened in their version, whether it's true or false. And who knows, they may say something stupid! Obviously, they can't lie about everything or the likelihood they could prevail would be quite slim.

So, Mr. Quinn lived to regret informing me that this was a tactic to use when dealing with people whom you suspect will be giving false testimony . . . and I used it! Now you may understand why Mr. Quinn was so red in the face. Turnabout is fair play, don't you think? But in this case, it sure was a low blow to Mr. Quinn's demeanor. You should have seen the three cocky attorneys, their heads were tipped and their eyes were looking down into their computers as if they were looking for answers.

Not only was his face redder than fruit punch, he answered the Arbitrator's and my questions like we were drill sergeants in a military boot camp drill. If there was any satisfaction, I mean any infinitesimal tiny amount of satisfaction out of this entire process of filing fraud charges against an attorney and still losing, this had to be one notable moment in attempting to bring justice to Darren Quinn. Yep, you could say, I certainly succeeded in vexing Mr. Quinn for a few good moments and I was there to bear witness to the occasion. It was costly, but it was sweet.

I proceeded to make a point in the hearing with the Arbitrator and, I'd like to clarify with you, the readers . . . just how did this whole mess come about?

In early 2000, I wanted to inspect some corporate records of the company I'd had suspicions of foul play, and I gave Mr. Quinn $500 to draft a letter on March 2, 2000, requesting minutes of board meetings, profit and loss status, etc. Additionally however, Mr. Quinn chose to include the following last paragraph to the request letter:

> Unless this issue is resolved very quickly, you can expect the next documents you will receive concerning this matter to be a summons and complaint. ABC will, of course, be ultimately liable for the filing fees and costs to serve the summons and complaint.

In arbitration, I asked Mr. Quinn, "Do you recall if I was a happy or unhappy investor with ABC company about that time of February of 2000?"

He answered, "Unhappy because they couldn't get certain documents and information that they wanted."

Then I asked Mr. Quinn, "Does that last paragraph threaten ABC in any way, shape, or form that you would threaten to file a lawsuit?"

And Mr. Quinn answered, "It threatens a lawsuit."

So I then asked Mr. Quinn, "Does threatening a lawsuit generally indicate an adversarial relationship in most circumstances between yourself and/or represented clients and the company you are threatening, as in this letter?"

He answered, "Litigation is adversarial."

Let me clarify that the greatest fraud in this underlying case went down in the next few months following this exchange of well-chosen words by Mr. Quinn, who admitted, he threatened the very company I wished to request documents from. Mr. Quinn pissed off the ABC company people with his threatening letter and they retaliated. For my own declaration here, I wasn't interested in a lawsuit and I told Mr. Quinn we did not want to be drawn into anything of the sort. I would argue profusely, yes, Mr. Quinn by his own vexing, initiated this whole stinking nightmare. I didn't first approach Mr. Quinn and request he file a lawsuit, I simply wanted documents. The difference here is that business people want facts to do their job; attorneys want lawsuits to do theirs, and they will go to great extents to start one. I'd have never been dragged into this whole mess if it had not been for Mr. Darren J. Quinn.

I asked Mr. Quinn, "Mr. Quinn, did this case that you filed on March 22, 2001, involve fraud?"

He answered, "It was alleged to involve fraud, yes."

I asked, "Was this case regarding ABC—was this packed with fraud, Mr. Quinn?"

He answered, "Packed with alleged fraud."

I asked, "Did you believe it?"

He answered, "It wasn't really passing the lawyer smell test, . . . And so that—it never seemed to make sense to me, but I'm obligated to believe what they say. So I did, and I argued it, and that's what I did."

I seem to recall from being at the hearing that Mr. Quinn specifically answered, "Yes." But the record specifically doesn't reflect that answer. Obviously, my recollection was incorrect.

Now how and why would an attorney file a claim for fraud, allege fraud in the complaint, pack the complaint with fraud, tell the jury upon opening remarks that this is a picture of fraud, prepare exhibits #93 and #94 which are admissions to fraud for two defendants and ask the judge to enter them as evidence, obtain a $660,000 judgment against a defendant for fraud, and make claims that other defendants are now linked to the "dirtiest of them all," and under oath state, "it wasn't really passing the lawyer smell test and it never seemed to make sense to me"?

Is Mr. Quinn then guilty of filing a frivolous claim knowingly from the start? How can you ask the court for a default judgment on one hand and claim it doesn't pass the smell test on the other? Does anyone sense a little discontinuity of judicial professionalism? Just a tiny bit?

I asked Mr. Quinn, "Did this case involve conspiracy fraud?"

He answered, "It is my practice to have the conspiracy allegation in this complaint. There was one in this one."

I asked, "Was anyone prosecuted in this case, Mr. Quinn?"

He answered, "Not that I know of."

I asked, "Did anyone go to jail?"

He answered, "Not that I know of."

Regarding the trial exhibits #93 and #94 which Mr. Quinn turned into the court and that he intended to use, I asked him: "Do they state that literally all the defendants in this case had committed fraud?"

He answered, "Probably, I was reasonably thorough." That's what every client likes to hear!

I asked, "Ok, this is a powerful document, is it not, Mr. Quinn?"

He answers, "Powerful if it gets into evidence. It's powerful to the extent it says those requests are deemed admitted. It is powerful."

I asked, "What did you do with the court order?"

He answered, "The court order stays in the file."

I asked, "Did you communicate this court order to us plaintiffs, Kennan Kaeder, or the judge about the next entire 11 months of this case?"

He answers, "Kennan Kaeder was aware of it."

We heard Mr. Kaeder's testimony who claimed he was sandbagged and Mr. Quinn answered the judge directly about having sent Mr. Kaeder a formal notice—by replying with a, "No." Seems to me that somebody is lying. How about you?

On one of the most important pieces of evidence riding on the entire lawsuit, Mr. Quinn puts the order in the file and admits he does not send Mr. Kaeder a formal notice of it, yet claims 5–6 years later that Mr. Kaeder was aware of it. I'm not buying it.

I must say though, I am so grateful for the fact that Mr. Quinn and his partner Mr. DeCicco, presumably hired and paid for the court recorder at their expense to be there and record everything that was said during the hearing so it could be transcribed into transcripts. All I had to do was contact the court recorder and pay her to transcribe the hearing and send me a copy so I have legal recorded documents from the hearing. Thanks guys; money well spent!

"You seem to have more than the average share of intelligence for a man of your background," sneered the lawyer at a witness on the stand.

"If I wasn't under oath, I'd return the compliment," replied the witness.

I used those very transcripts to provide quoted statements by everyone there including the Arbitrator. And just to clarify how this all works for folks who have never set foot in a lawsuit, I could never say or list anything that I heard Mr. Quinn, Mr. DeCicco, or the Arbitrator say in this book without the legal hearing recordings or anyone in the legal profession could and most certainly would declare everything I said they said to be "HEARSAY." And the value of anything I said they said would be considered untruthful and not credible evidence and could never be used or taken to be the truth. Oh, they would love to sue me if I were lying, right?

So, with that being said, Mr. Quinn and Mr. DeCicco inadvertently provided me with one of the most valuable judicial tools enabling me to broadcast the exact words of their actions to you. They may not like it, but that is an uncalculated risk they took when they chose to hire the court recorder for this hearing. Once done, it cannot be undone.

I am free to use the exact quotations for you to witness what was said without you having to have been there to verify it. Again, for this little token of effort, I'd like to give special thanks for one form of the judicial system that works quite well. I understand even this system of recording what people say is not 100 percent perfectly accurate, but it usually can be considered in the high 90s percentage of being accurate and the judicial system relies heavily upon recorded transcripts as the gospel truth as to what happened at and during that setting.

Did you hear about the new sushi bar that caters exclusively to lawyers?
It's called Sosumi.

During the arbitration hearing, there was one head shaking experience after another. There we were, during the first day of arbitration, we hadn't been back from lunch very long and the Arbitrator announces:

So let's do this: Can we take a break? I need to do a quick teleconference for another arbitration that's totally unavoidable. I wish I could have reset it. But could you do this for me: I do want to hear more on this point. And I'll return to you Mr. Schuelke, and we can talk about this further. Okay? Thank you very much, folks. I would like for you and Mr. Schuelke to finish your presentations today. Okay. Fair enough?

And a recess was taken.

I had paid for and expected one and a half days to put on my evidence and after Mr. DeCicco finally got done rambling in the morning, there was hardly any time for me to put on my evidence. Now the Arbitrator is asking for me to be thinking about finishing already today. Sitting there dismayed, I had to wonder just what kind of justice is this? This is why Mr. Quinn purposely tucked in that arbitration clause in his retainer agreement that if any disputes arise, we must settle our dispute outside of courthouse rules.

As a matter for the record, the Arbitrator left and was gone for nearly 3 hours.

This was crucial time I needed to put on my 283 pages of evidence and we had not even scratched the surface of the facts I had prepared to cover. I was not happy. The Arbitrator wanted us to finish presentations today! I thought, no way. I paid big money for this Arbitration process and he wanted it done after what little time was left after DeCicco was done ranting before noon and now this!

Well, if I were to say things were about to go to hell in a hand basket, it's because they were!

It didn't help either that the Arbitrator was gone, out of the room, and the clock on the wall was indicating my allotted presentation time was vanishing fast. I was thinking, *how am I going to do this?*

Once the Arbitrator returned, the answer to my previous question was soon given. His first words were no more than a mere continuance of a steady process conveniently established to kill my evidence. His words struck me like being hit by a baseball bat. I felt like I was railroaded from the blind side and struck totally numb when he made an announcement right after he returned from his long absence:

> I feel an interim ruling of the Arbitrator based on the evidence at least to the point is in the process—it strikes me that given that there's no legal standard of care, expert testimony, being proffered by the counterclaimants here and with this really being a case that truly sounds in legal malpractice, that I'm going to limit the presentation of the evidence from this point forward only to such remaining evidence that Mr. Schuelke would like to offer relative to intentional misrepresentations or fraud.

> But anything else in relation to whether or not strategic considerations of whether or not there has been negligence on the part of Mr. Quinn, I don't find to be relevant because we simply have no legal expert on that. What I will do, though, starting tomorrow morning—what I'd like to do is continue this process that we began, which is I'm going to look at the documents tonight. Mr. Schuelke, I'm going to have specific items that I'd like you to address. If it's okay with you, Mr. DeCicco, if I can just continue the way we're doing it.

And of course Mr. DeCicco answered, "That's fine."

The Arbitrator turned to me and further stated,

> But it's just one of those cases, Mr. Schuelke, where this is a case that absolutely cries for expert testimony because the law just basically says that a layperson can't opine with what's called legal competence on whether or not an attorney has met his or her standard of care in terms of development of the case.

> And given the fact that an attorney cannot ethically guarantee results is very difficult to kind of, after the fact, Monday morning quarterback and then

show what could have happened, or should have happened, absent expert testimony to show that the standard of care has been complied with.

So, you still have an opportunity to present to me with evidence on the fraud. But in terms of any other claims sounding in professional negligence, professional malpractice, you don't have any competent expert testimony to offer me to substantiate those claims. As a matter of law, they would have to fail. All right?

Other than that, I feel I made the right ruling on the Statute of Limitations. This case is about fraud. There's an exception under 3340.6 for fraud. So I am happy that I did allow you to go forward on your fraud claims in that regard. I don't find that the case is time-barred by the Statute of Limitations because of the express statutory carve-out, if you will for fraud.

But I'm very, very convinced that for professional negligence or anything short of just fraudulent conduct, that the law just clearly requires expert testimony on that.

So, my evidence was totally worthless to him because I wasn't an attorney. Anything that I said or could say was not to be trusted. I needed to pay another attorney to be present to say what I was prepared to say so Mr. Coleman, the arbitrator, could believe it was based on coming from someone from a far superior world of knowledge. You heard it: "As a matter of law," my evidence and testimony would fail because it didn't come out of the mouth of another attorney. Gee, that's funny folks, because before this whole arbitration process took place I went on the arbitration website and printed off all, and I mean all, the rules and regulations for arbitration, and I didn't find any such law or laws! There was not one word about having to have an expert witness for my case. An Arbitrator obviously isn't smart enough to be able to decide or render a decision on his own whether or not evidence exists so they have to rely on someone else's opinion. How's that for a joke?

What's the difference between a Lawyer and a Liar?

The pronunciation.

Then the Arbitrator turns to Mr. Quinn and states, "It's your call as to whether or not you want Mr. Pettit, your expert witness, involved tomorrow in light of my ruling." (Mr. Pettit was Mr. Quinn's expert witness, hired by Mr. Quinn to give so-called expert testimony on behalf of Mr. Quinn, describing the quality of Mr. Quinn's service.)

Mr. Quinn: "He has opinions on the reasonableness of the fees. If it makes sense to take it briefly out of order to have him talk about that, we could. Or I can bring him back tomorrow."

The Arbitrator: "Well, I need Mr. Schuelke's concurrence first because it's still part of your presentation on the fraud claims."

Mr. Quinn: "We'll just bring him back. Don't worry about it."

Then the Arbitrator had one last thing he wanted to say for the day, "So your case won't be interrupted, you'll lead off tomorrow morning. Ok, thank you very much. I appreciate everybody's professionalism here today. It really helped me to understand things. My apologies again for that delay. I had some things to deal with."

That ended day one of Arbitration. I call this a good, old-fashioned raping. I was slapped in the face procedurally and so belittlingly by the Arbitrator and struck down by such an "interim ruling" because I was a layperson and my evidence just "cries for expert testimony" and was not even going to be considered as a result! Yet I was expressly thanked for sitting and taking this like a professional? The word rape does list one of its definitions as any gross violation, assault, or abuse. I think it does apply here!

I was so stunned by this event, I most normally would have had a response, but it was so bad, as I said, I was numbed and literally speechless. So this was the "Due Process" Mr. Coleman spoke of in our first preliminary hearing that he said I was entitled to. This was the demonstrated open, more lenient forum he spoke of, compared to the more strict and procedural oriented state court formal trial process which certainly did require having an attorney to represent you. In this case, having an attorney to represent me obviously would have made zero difference.

I started gathering up my things to go back to the hotel for the evening. I spent months on the process of preparing for this hearing, gathering the truth. I had about 30 pages of formalized questions to ask Mr. Quinn. I spent an unrealistic amount of money in copy costs, binders, special order tabs, postal costs, hotel costs, airfare, car rental, gas, meals, etc., in addition to the hearing fees, to be told my evidence just couldn't be considered. You have no idea what that does to your soul.

The evidence was in the arbitrator's hands and one of the most sickening comments was he had never even looked at it. Although he promised he would look at it before tomorrow, the last day.

This is the same Arbitrator who told me in the first preliminary hearing I did not need to be represented by an attorney and I did not have to have an expert witness to present my case, and then he makes this interim ruling barring my evidence. Does this look like a set up or what? Does anyone feel a hint of extortion here? He later in his ruling admits there was discussion on this very subject. Now, I have good reason to not trust the Arbitrator because he told me something different during the first preliminary hearing just so we could move forward with this formal and quite expensive process.

Don't you think for just one minute that if he had, in fact, told me the truth that my evidence could not be considered without an expert, that I wouldn't have been so stupid to spend the money, prepare, and travel 2,000 miles to knowingly have my evidence banned from being considered? Is this just one of the facets of the modern-day judicial system standard of care powers of an arbitrator that they possess and utilize at their disposal?

I called the very attorney who filed the case for me and he was unavailable for the day, so I left a message as to what happened. By the time I heard back from him, the damage had already been done.

All I could do was head out for a good meal and try to relax for a few hours and clear my head. The day unraveled not quite the way I expected it to. But, that's the way everyone says arbitration goes. About the only consolation I received that first day was on one of the breaks when the court recorder asked me if I had done this before and I told her no. She told me I was really doing a good job.

After dinner, I spent a couple of hours pouring over my questions to direct my presentation according to the arbitrator's ruling and I needed some way to address this interim ruling. I finally grew tired and tried getting a good night's sleep. You can imagine how that went.

We started the next and last day, pretty much the same way as the first day. I arrived first and was refreshed and ready to go. And sure enough, the defense wasn't one minute early. It seemed to me as though they prided themselves on not being punctual and instead wanted to delay every crucial minute so as to reduce the available hearing time. And it worked again.

Once we were underway and the court recorder was doing her thing, the arbitrator stated, "we're back on the record" and I had to challenge his last ruling some way or another, so I asked the Arbitrator,

> Regarding your interim ruling yesterday, I would like to have a little discussion, if I could, on that. My understanding is, on the first preliminary hearing, I remember DeCicco—Mr. DeCicco making mention that an expert witness was required, and we had discussion about that.
>
> And you had said that at that point in time that it wasn't absolutely essential and we could go on. And you said that an expert witness, you know, would lend credibility in the case, but we could move forward, withstanding that.
>
> And your decision yesterday—I had basically gotten not quite one-third through of my evidence, and you made this ruling and that thus bars me to be able to provide any evidence regarding malpractice. And I would like to— based on that, I would like to request a continuance until such time we could reconvene and continue with an expert witness.

I also told him his ruling was extremely prejudicial by not allowing me to present my evidence on malpractice and that this is a very serious matter, which affects me and my family in regards to moneys we have worked for all our lives. I told him it would be a gross miscarriage of justice to allow this to proceed without having a chance to present all of the evidence in this case and have it considered.

The Arbitrator replied, "The problem with that is that it is terribly prejudicial to the other party, who has prepared for the hearing and it delays things even more. And once it's kind of game day, we have to go forward and then that presents all kinds of problems in terms of basically abuse of process."

Well, who knows more about abuse of process and delaying the process of justice than attorneys? It was OK for Mr. Quinn to schedule multiple hearing dates for taking a defendants deposition with delays. It was OK for Mr. Quinn to delay/sandbag evidence 11 months prior to trial while Mr. Quinn could charge me for all the total time, travel time, and so forth. So, why was it when I needed to reschedule for something as crucial as this, I am denied? There's no dual standard; it's just a figment of my imagination.

In fact, the Arbitrator was so kind to cite the ruling he made to make me feel better:

> All right. I'm going to read from the Commercial Arbitration Rules and Mediation Procedures, dated July 1, 2003, which are the rules that are in effect for this particular arbitration since they were the ones that were effective at the time the claim was filed.

> Rule 30-B; Conduct of Proceedings: "The arbitrator exercising his or her discretion shall conduct the proceedings with a view to expediting the resolution of the dispute—it mandates that I should conduct the proceedings with a view towards expediting this and for me to direct the parties to produce or to present in a way that can dispose of all or part of the case."

Then he repeats himself again, saying, "I owe it to this process, in the spirit of expedition, to let you know I don't believe I can legally give much weight to your presentation and your evidence on standard of care because you can't competently—in the legalese, competently testify or offer evidence on that without an expert. So I owe it to the process to let you know that I think the interim ruling is appropriate because there's no way I could in fairness give much weight." So let's just apply the arbitration system's ornate authorized rules and dispose of all or part of the case, shall we?

Since this determination was made that I was not qualified to submit evidence of my findings, I immediately thought of a way around this. I thought I would find out if even a judge is considered to be an expert in his mind. I'm fairly confident the Arbitrator never even so much as sifted through my 283 pages of incriminating evidence against Mr. Quinn. I'll pose this one to you; I'll cite what the judge said while being critical of Mr. Quinn's actions: "As I've indicated before gentlemen, I've got the paucity of law in this case. I've never been faced with this situation. Fifteen years on the bench, I've never been faced with this situation."

Let's properly define the word paucity as *Webster's Dictionary* lists:

> **Paucity:** *1. Smallness of number or quantity. 2 Scarcity; insufficiency.*

I most certainly wanted the Arbitrator to know about an event Mr. Quinn had to be very concerned with regarding fraud at our hearing. Mr. Quinn delayed my case for more years of litigation on appeal in pursuit of $2.7 million in damages against Mr. Tim Connor. This all sounded like quite a masterful windfall deal, but the only problem was that I found out after the years of waiting for this, Mr. Quinn had orchestrated another round of chess. In the underlying case, there was documented talk by Mr. Quinn of the existence of an insurance policy, which was to be the restitution source for making me whole as the result of the fraud involved. If I was to get a judgment against Tim Connor, the insurance policy would pay the damages; or at least that is what Mr. Quinn led me to believe.

So during the hearing discussion the Arbitrator asked me, "Basically, what you're just saying is that there was a representation that there was insurance money available to satisfy a judgment—is that right?"

I had explained this was the representation Mr. Quinn gave me to lead me to believe there was an insurance policy and I did have documented e-mails with Mr. Quinn providing reference to Mr. Quinn's representation that a policy existed.

The Arbitrator stated, and this is *huge*,

> when, in fact, there wasn't? Well, I think in a broader scope, I think it lends to an ethical responsibility when you provide legal representation—I may be wrong on this, but if there are not grounds or no possibilities of recovery and you're giving a false statement to a client that a policy exists that you can utilize to not only get your compensatory, but a huge, fabricated $2.7 million judgment, I call that a very fraudulent representation to us when we found out later that it didn't exist. Is that your testimony that representation was made to you?

I replied, "Yes."

My proof was well documented in my three-inch three ring binder of evidence and it was in tab number 12, bates number 00090. This was right before the arbitrator, Mr. Harold Coleman's, very eyes.

This was an e-mail I kept from Mr. Quinn where he stated, "I spoke with Mike Brown (Connor's old defense attorney). He said Don McVey had a copy of the insurance policies. I left a message for Don McVey."

Proof of an insurance policy in existence would better justify pursuing a lawsuit, hoping to collect from the insurance policy. If there was, in fact, no insurance policy, the likelihood of collecting was a crapshoot.

In a previous e-mail I asked Mr. Quinn, "How much time can it take to ascertain the insurance policy?"

Then on page 00092 of tab #12, I asked, "Darren, just wondering if you'd heard anything back from McVey concerning Tim's insurance policy?"

Mike Brown was listed as one of my witnesses and I asked to have him called to testify, which we did over the phone.

Once on the phone, I asked Mr. Brown, "Do you recall Darren Quinn having any discussions with you regarding your client, as you were representing Tim Connor, that an insurance policy existed covering Mr. Connor for his actions on behalf of this A.B.C. lawsuit?"

Mr. Brown responded saying, "No, I have no recollection of any discussions, personal recollections of that, no. I would say that if I had had discussions about an insurance policy, I'm certain that we would have tendered the insurance policy to the insurance carrier."

I asked, "For what purpose, Mr. Brown?"

Mr. Brown answered, "To pick up the cost of defense because Mr. Connor was paying out of his pocket to defend this matter, and it got to be expensive. And that's eventually why we had to withdraw from his representation, was because he just couldn't afford us. If he had an insurance policy, we definitely would have tendered the defense of this claim to the insurance carrier."

Mr. Quinn testified, "It wasn't produced in litigation. There was no insurance policy that I ever saw or that was ever produced, but there was certainly discussion of it. And I relayed those discussions to the Schuelkes."

Mr. Quinn also testified, "What I did is—we've been trying to figure out what Mr. Schuelke's case was about. So once he provided his binder, then it gave more detail. Then it looks like it may be an insurance issue. So I tried to—"

And Mr. DeCicco cut off Mr. Quinn and said, "We prepared for the conversation."

Do you have any idea what just went on here? You can judge!

Well, that was about the gist of it. Mr. Quinn and Mr. DeCicco wanted the arbitrator to know that Mr. Quinn was just simply relaying second-hand information he was getting so that he was not purposely telling me wrong or incorrect information. Shoot, he is only an attorney. He couldn't have possibly known whether or not a policy actually existed. It would have been far too prudent and too much work for an attorney handling a case to ascertain or obtain a copy of it first before we set out for a pot of gold worth $2.7 million bucks.

Was this fraud, or was Mr. Brown just lying? Let me help you here—Mr. Brown was telling the truth. Again, the arbitrator stated earlier, "I call that a very fraudulent representation" if the elements existed as he first understood my complaint. One thing was for certain . . . an insurance policy never existed. I thought I made my point perfectly clear; there certainly was talk of an insurance policy by Mr. Quinn and I thought I made my point that it didn't actually exist. I also thought that ought to suffice with the arbitrator, but obviously I was mistaken.

During the hearing, I gave Mr. Quinn the golden opportunity to clear his name and bury me for once and for all on the fraud charges. I made him an offer that could have acquitted him from the entire hearing. I said, "And I'll tell you what. I'll be willing to shorten this thing up today. If Darren Quinn and DeCicco can show me in the next 14 days after October 26, 2001—if they can show that the ABC defendants responded to that 14-day request and he filed a motion for summary judgment against the defendants, I'll be willing to drop our fraud charges against Darren Quinn."

There wasn't anything on the record that shows whether they were able to produce either one. And would you believe, I seem to recall the arbitrator asking Mr. Quinn and Mr. DiCicco, "Can you?" But again, there seems to be a void in the record here. There seemed to be quite a few other places in the record where I recalled Mr. Quinn providing specific answers but the record just didn't seem to reflect my recollection. Now, I have to wonder whether I had memory issues or had the arbitration hearing transcripts somehow been altered?

What do honest lawyers and UFOs have in common?

You always hear about them, but you never see them.

You see, when I called the deposition service after the arbitration hearing and informed them I wanted transcripts of the hearing they told me it normally takes a week and a half to produce them. I found it a little strange that this time, it took a month. I also asked them for a copy of the tapes so I could make my own verifications for correctness and I was told the tapes weren't available. I also asked to have a copy of the corrections that were made to the transcripts by the other party and I was told there weren't any corrections, period. I asked if they were sure about that and I was told there were no corrections. I also asked to speak directly with Sharon Susa, the court recorder herself, and I wanted to hear it from her that there had been no changes or corrections made to the transcripts and she was off limits to any communication whatsoever. I even tracked down her cell phone number and called and left messages to her phone and she would not return my call. The company responded by saying they acknowledged that I called Sharon and they informed me that I could not speak with her. But yet I spoke with two of the court recorders who recorded the September 2001 trial hearing. I wonder why I couldn't communicate with the court recorder that Mr. Quinn and Mr. DeCicco hired to record the arbitration hearing. Do you suppose Mr. Quinn and Mr. DeCicco actually worked with the recorded transcripts and made many changes and didn't want anyone to know about it?

I seem to recall at the end of the hearing Mr. Coleman asked Mr. Quinn how much per hour he was charging clients currently and I recalled Mr. Quinn giving him an answer, but there was no record of that either. Obviously, the records show my recollections were incorrect.

Mr. Quinn had me make corrections to my deposition recordings. And I received copies of those corrections from that court recorder.

Maybe someday someone can take the initiative to investigate Mr. Quinn and Mr. DeCicco as to whether or not Sharon Susa or her company made any changes to the original arbitration recordings. I certainly would like to see the result.

Oddly enough, I also requested a copy of the recorded tapes that Mr. Harold Coleman took also during the arbitration hearing and the case manager Lisa Allen-Cumiford told me I could not get a copy of those either.

Once I started fighting fire with fire by using the DiFiglias' comments as expert opinions regarding Mr. Quinn's performances, we worked ourselves into a discussion where fur was about to fly. I was getting somewhere and the defense wasn't liking it. I could tell Mr. Arbitrator wasn't either. The heat was near a boiling point when we were discussing the unanswered interrogatories in which Mr. Quinn attempted to ban the defendants from providing testimony at trial. I used the quote from the judge where he is in question as to whether or not to exercise his power to set aside Mr. Quinn's motion to admit the defendants' own admission of guilt. That obviously was one up on the arbitrator.

You don't have to be an attorney to be able to detect a slight degree of human discomfort when someone is in a pickle. Guilty minds tend to show some emotion on the exterior like breaking away from eye contact, lowering the chin and eyes, twitching a shoulder, or changing the question. I knew I had done my job from the reactions I witnessed from the arbitrator. If you've ever raised children, you know what I'm talking about. The same principle applies to adults. Adults just have the ability to get into stickier situations and those same human reactions are just sometimes too hard to contain.

The next move by the arbitrator was at the core of the juggernaut defense system. I had Mr. Quinn backed into a corner and their escape from their own defense was impossible. Mr. DeCicco couldn't help him either.

So, the arbitrator says, "All right, Mr. DeCicco, I am going to do something simply because I have the power to do it." Doesn't this subliminally seem to say, "OK, watch this boys"?

Then the arbitrator turns to Mr. Pettit, and asks, "Would you raise your right hand?" . . . and proceeds to swear in Mr. Quinn's so-called expert witness.

"You are here on behalf of Mr. Quinn today as an expert witness; correct, sir?"

Mr. Pettit answers, "Yes. A better way to phrase that would be I've defended attorneys in various professional liability type claims. I've tried numerous cases. I've tried fraud cases, conspiracy cases. I haven't been an expert for all that time."

In the aftermath, I'm thinking, *So is he an expert or is he not? I must be one now, too!*

The arbitrator asks, "You've heard the testimony of Mr. Quinn in its entirety? Give me your professional opinion in this regard."

Mr. Pettit had been sitting in on the hearing up until this time and had not said a word. He had been the best example of Little Miss Bo Peep you ever saw.

He now responded with a battery of blurbs like: "You know, based on what I've seen, I think it was excellent. I mean just looking over all the case as a whole, I think Mr. Quinn from my view—put his client in a position to achieve a settlement in a case where the trial did not go as well as they hoped it would . . . I think the criticisms about the trial are absurd . . . Just looking solely at that issue, I think the way Mr. Quinn handled that was completely appropriate."

Regarding the interrogatories: "Instead, Mr. Quinn took, I think, a very—took the right approach to it, brought it up at trial at a point where Judge DiFiglia is now saying, 'I might be powerless to set aside these requests for admissions and even points out this is akin to a default.' But in terms of a tort, I think Mr. Quinn's analysis was right on . . . And finally, given the settlement, there's no relevance anyway . . . Again, I mean given the circumstances at the time, it certainly seems to be a fair settlement."

And his final assessment, "And I think claims that somehow there was a breach of the standard of care are totally and completely without merit."

The arbitrator asked Mr. Pettit, "So is there anything that you are able to discern from the record from your review in this case that would suggest that Mr. Quinn was less than candid or in some way may have misled the plaintiffs in relation to the discussions that resulted in their approval of the settlement?"

He replied, "No, not at all. Certainly, we'd have to assume Mr. Schuelke took those representations with a grain of salt given the fact that his entire claim was one for fraud."

The arbitrator even went so far as to audaciously ask Mr. Pettit, "In your professional opinion, given what the court apparently said on the record in terms of there's no evidence of fraud, are you at all critical of Mr. Quinn having actually brought this suit on behalf of the underlying plaintiffs based upon fraud?"

And, of course, Mr. Pettit answered . . . you guessed it, "No."

The arbitrator said, "Thank you very much, I might have more questions for you later."

Indeed, later he asks Mr. Pettit, "Expert Pettit, give me your opinion on this. Should Mr. Quinn have pled $2.7 million in damages in either the initial complaint or the first amended complaint?"

Mr. Pettit responded with, "Well, I feel the complaint was adequately pled. He met the standard of care . . . I think Mr. Quinn did the right thing in pursuing a higher damage claim. It puts more pressure on the defendants.

You're lucky if you get it—the incremental cost was justified to pursue it. So I didn't find a breach of the standard of care."

Are you surprised by Mr. Pettit's responses so far?

The arbitrator asked Mr. Pettit: "In conducting your review and evaluation of the file and circumstances surrounding this particular arbitration claim, did you see anything that made you feel as though the case had been over-litigated?"

Mr. Pettit answered, "No. Just the opposite. I mean, this would—this would go into the opinion I would give on the billing statements, and I won't get into that completely . . . I thought it was unbelievably—really unbelievably reasonable to get that much done with that kind of fee . . . Everything seemed to be related to pursuing the case, obtaining a judgment, and benefiting the client."

Well now, you heard it. Mr. Quinn didn't charge me enough! He should have charged me even more for what he got accomplished! I should be grateful for all his benefits to me as a client and maybe it sounds like a gratuitous tip would even be in order, huh? How could I be so shallow minded not to be more appreciative of Mr. Quinn's accomplishments? After all, Mr. Quinn obtained a judgment, called a default judgment, against the one individual who didn't even come to trial to defend himself, now I call that a monster accomplishment by any attorney terms. Even though that individual didn't receive the money that was fraudulently taken, he got paid a $30,000 commission for his role and he is on the hook for the entire enchilada. Now, that's justice in the purest sense, is it not?

Experts are people who know a great deal about very little and who go along learning more and more about less and less until they know practically everything about nothing.

Lawyers, on the other hand, are people who know very little about many things and keep learning less and less about more and more until they know practically nothing about everything.

The arbitrator: "And then in looking at the entire case and the documents that you reviewed, what's your opinion of the quality of the communication, the written communication, from Mr. Quinn to the Schuelkes in keeping them informed of the developments in the case and so forth?"

Mr. Pettit: "I thought it was excellent."

Although the insurance policy Quinn touted didn't exist . . . even though Mr. Quinn represented there was one, he didn't have the guts to tell me we lost the $2.7 million dollar claim he had "fabricated" according to the arbitrators' own term. I was informed by someone else. Mr. Quinn can deny he had any obligation to tell me directly why he lost this massive claim in both the state court and the appeal court rulings. Yet, Mr. Expert Witness says this is excellent communication. I'd call that "professional" representation at its finest!

Cowardice is evidently also no criteria in the standard of care when it comes to properly informing your client why you were "incrementally" charged years worth of more attorney fees to argue why I was entitled to this huge claim, and lose.

The Arbitrator: "Have you seen anything or evaluated anything in doing your work in this case that would lead you to believe that Mr. Quinn had deceived his client?"

Mr. Pettit: "No. Absolutely not."

The Arbitrator: "Thinking back on everything you reviewed in preparing your opinions and the testimony you've heard over the last day and a half in this arbitration, is there anything at all that would opine that could have, should have been done differently by Mr. Quinn?"

Mr. Pettit: "No."

The Arbitrator: "Okay, All right. Mr. Schuelke, that does it for me in terms of what I think I need. Any further questions that we need to explore?"

Mr. Schuelke: "I'd like to ask one question. Are you being paid to attend this arbitration hearing by Mr. Quinn and Mr. DeCicco?"

Mr. Pettit: "I certainly expect to be."

Now, I do believe that to be a true answer and statement. Only one thing seems to strike me strange here was I seemed to recall asking Mr. Pettit how much and what the agreement was for and the record doesn't reflect an answer. Obviously, my recollection, again, was incorrect.

Then I had one last question for Mr. Pettit: "You also saw the judge's comments regarding at the tail-end of the trial, the miscarriage of justice. Is that your opinion too—in contrary to Judge DiFiglia in this case? You're saying contrary, Mr. Quinn's performance was excellent, and the judge stated there was a miscarriage of justice. Are you stating your opinion overstates the opinion of the judge who orchestrated and resided over the case at trial?"

Mr. Pettit: "Well, Mr. Schuelke, you and I interpret the judge's comments differently. So—I don't disagree with the judge because I interpret his comments differently than you do."

Well, I'd say we finally came to some form of agreement. We agree we interpret something differently. Now, I'd say we were making progress. Oh, but Mr. Pettit was quite a wiggle worm when I asked him further pinpoint questions, like:

Mr. Schuelke: "And you also heard Mr. Quinn testify yesterday when I asked Mr. Quinn directly if he alleged fraud. And then I asked him did he believe we were defrauded, and he answered, yes. Isn't that correct?"

Mr. Pettit: "I'm not sure if that was the exact testimony or not. I don't want to say something because I don't recall exactly."

How could this have happened? He was sitting in the same room with us and now the "Expert" doesn't recall the previous day? Isn't it amazing how attorneys can remember what they choose to and they just can't recall what they don't want admitted into evidence as the truth?

Since he appeared to like dancing around the truth, I decided to crank up the tunes so everybody could dance. I wanted to pin him down and bust his chops so I asked him this:

Mr. Schuelke: "Okay, for the record, Mr. Quinn did answer that he did believe that the Schuelkes were defrauded on behalf of the defendants, Okay? Based on that testimony that Mr. Quinn gave yesterday, is it your professional opinion that justice was served knowing today, as we sit in this arbitration hearing today, that again Thomas Carter, Joe Lindquist, or John Cole—none of those have returned any of that money knowing that Mr. Quinn alleged fraud, he believes there's fraud—are you saying as an expert witness today that you believe justice was served against those defendants?"

Mr. Pettit: "Well, it's not—"

Mr. DeCicco: "I'm going to put an objection on relevancy grounds. It's kind of beyond the scope."

The Arbitrator: "So noted. He can handle it. Mr. Pettit, go ahead."

Mr. Pettit: "Part of what I was going to say, Mr. Schuelke, I'm not necessarily agreeing with everything you've asked or built into your question. My role, though, was not to determine whether justice was served in the underlying case. My role was to say what kind of work did Mr. Quinn do on your behalf? Are the fees reasonable? Did he do anything that breached the standard of care? And those are things I'm talking about."

I'm just asking this expert a direct question! Do you get the feeling that attorneys answer only the questions they want to answer since they "feel" they have a "role" to play and specific issues are selectively out of their "scope" in the process? I guess I was just asking him questions that were not pertaining to what he was being paid to say, was I? Selective judicial bargaining, I call it. Maybe I should have offered to pay him to answer the question better for me, suppose? Maybe I should have asked him if I paid him, would he then answer my question truthfully? I do wonder how he would have answered that.

Mr. Schuelke: "Well, you are rendering your opinion—"

Mr. Pettit: "The question of whether justice was served vis-à-vis the underlying defendants is really a difficult question for me to answer. If they defrauded you and they cheated you and your wife out of your money, the answer is no, justice was not served . . . I don't know. I didn't make the decision about what's justice . . . That's not something that I was hired to do, and that's not really something that I could do."

I don't believe much more needs to be said on this subject—an expert witness just selectively won't "make the decision" to determine whether or not justice is proper after reviewing a case . . . unless he is "hired" and paid enough. But he is certain here though, that an attorney's performance was "excellent" under these circumstances.

Mr. Quinn, like all attorneys, had supplied me with a contract agreement with associated terms. I would not agree to some of his terms and asked to have some removed and some modified. Like liens against my property; I asked him to remove this and he did. Once we arrived at a mutually agreeable retainer contract, we both signed it. To insure our costs on this matter would not escalate out of control, I drafted up a subsequent retainer agreement or letter of understanding, signed it, and forwarded it to Mr. Quinn. He didn't want to sign it, but I told him he could not proceed until he did. So he signed it and returned a copy to me.

This is where my dandruff, let's say, flared up. The whole case certainly should have stemmed from this very document alone, but never was considered to be anything but file 13 fodder. The agreement clearly stated how run-away legal fees were addressed. During the trial, I certainly didn't care to pay off the "run-away" legal fees Mr. Quinn chalked up for depositions for which he did not use one word of at trial. I didn't care to pay Mr. Quinn for his time obtaining the subpoenaed bank checks we found out we could not use at trial that Mr. Quinn illegally obtained because he didn't use a standard legal Notice of Privacy procedure. I didn't care to pay off the $1,600 he charged me for the muffed utilization of the Sanctions II software (remember I mentioned earlier about this computer interfaced overhead projector) that he experimented with for the first time, and I didn't care to pay off the bill he charged me for the lost and fabricated $2.7 million damages he claimed. I didn't care to pay off the bill for his incompetence in failing to commemorate properly the actual terms of the disastrous settlement like he said he would, and on and on. So, yes the bill did, for a long time, rise far above the referenced $5,000 amount in my/our signed last retainer agreement and we had an understanding about this. It was that if the bill grew larger than $5,000, he would have to get paid from any recovery he would obtain.

Obviously, this became an issue when Mr. Quinn, by his own incompetence, could not get paid off the modified recovery option. He then came back to me and wanted to be paid in full, plus interest. I simply expected what I believe any normal American citizen under these circumstances would have expected—some sort of appropriate and reasonable bill concession.

I certainly brought this up as the last thing at arbitration and here was Mr. DeCicco's response to this modified agreement: "If I received it and somebody said, Did you receive this? Did you get this notice? I'd say, Yes, I got the notice. Do I believe what's in the notice? Am I signing up for what's in the notice? No. I just got it. That's all the signature means, is that he (Mr. Quinn) received it and looked at it. It's not binding Mr. Quinn to anything."

Mr. Quinn even stated, "It was an acknowledgement of their financial situation and to be mindful of it."

This signed document/retainer agreement, which was the last agreement Mr. Quinn signed, never was considered or weighed in this arbitration process. Why? Because attorneys are above the law. They can sign documents that they draft and you are bound to them, but draft one yourself and have them sign it and it means they just received it and it doesn't mean a thing contractually.

I'd say fraud in the halls of justice just got away with a murder of my rights in the first degree. What's your take?

THE ATTORNEYS' PROBABILITY OF LYING TEST

1. *Pick a number from 1–9.*
2. *Multiply by 3.*
3. *Add 3.*
4. *Multiply by 3 again.*
5. *Now add the two digits of your answer together and match it up below to determine if you can predict the odds of attorneys lying to the public:*

    1. *The likelihood of finding one attorney who can change a light bulb.*
    2. *The chances an attorney could insert a square peg in a round hole.*
    3. *The chances you'll find skid marks on the road before a run over attorney.*
    4. *The likelihood an attorney will actually charge you less.*
    5. *The probability you will settle a case ahead of schedule.*
    6. *The likelihood you'll find an attorney chasing an ambulance without a broken nose.*
    7. *The likelihood of encouraging a trucking firm to contribute to an attorney's political campaign.*
    8. *The likelihood that only extremely important documents get lost in the mail.*
    9. *99.999999999999% of the time. We can't say they lie all the time because that would be lying. Barely.*
    10. *The chances of mustering the Trial Lawyers Association to host a tort reform rally.*

CHAPTER 6:

THE VERDICT

ON DECEMBER 7, 2007, as the hearing came to an end, the arbitrator finished with his kind words:

> And I want to thank both of you for your professionalism. I'm glad we were able to get it done in two days. Thanks for your flexibility in terms of the way you allowed me to vary the process so I could get what I need. I really appreciate your goodwill in that regard. But, I did want to make sure that Mr. Schuelke, who was unrepresented by counsel, did have a fair opportunity to present his evidence.
>
> Okay, other than that—let me say this just as a closing thought: You all strike me as really decent people. You really do. Every single person in this room.
>
> Conflict comes and conflicts goes. It's not a perfect system. We try as best we can. And there's no standard of perfection that is required anywhere. And I

just hope at the end of all of this, the parties will reflect back and can move forward with your respective lives. I certainly wish you well, Mr. Quinn, in your practice in the future, and you, Mr. Schuelke, with other things you may have going. I hope that you'll both in time—that a lot of this will abate and you can just reflect back and extract some lessons learned where necessary.

But, I think sometimes when people are embroiled in conflict—as a mediator, I see this so often—we sometimes tend to demonize the other party and think of the other party in terms of their worst motivations when, in reality, in many cases it's just a misunderstanding. Sometimes the misunderstanding is just borne of lack of knowledge of the process or the industry or whatever else.

And I'm just hoping that in time the parties can reflect and appropriately move on, move past this. Ok, again, my best to everyone here. Thank you very much.

"There's no standard of perfection that is required anywhere." Let's just consider this book an effort "to abate and reflect back and extract of some lessons learned where necessary," hopefully for the benefit of not only myself, but many others. Alright Mr. Arbitrator! Yes, let's do this. Nothing would make me happier than to be able to enlighten unsuspecting citizens that impartial courts like this exist in our judicial system today.

On December 19, 2007, the arbitrator signed his determination and forwarded his ruling . . . the verdict. Should it be no surprise that his ruling is summed up with these quotes?

The arbitrator hereby finds said fees to have been fair and reasonable, and necessary and proper to Claimant effectively representing Respondents' interests in the underlying securities fraud litigation and that no legal or factual justification exists for Respondents' failure to pay the balance due for the services rendered. The Arbitrator further finds that the evidence abundantly substantiates the fact that Claimant rendered his services honestly, competently, and in good faith, with Respondents' best interests in mind and in accordance with the requisite legal standards of care. The total sum awarded includes pre-award interest totaling $21,323.29 on the principal balance of $62,590.91. The Arbitrator hereby finds the said interest to be fair and reasonable under the circumstances.

Claimant in no manner defrauded or deceived Respondents in his representation.

Claimant proferred competent and persuasive expert testimony in establishing that his work in all respects complied with the requisite legal standards of care and the governing ethical canons. Claimant in fact secured a favorable judgment for Respondent in the underlying securities-fraud litigation that ultimately precipitated this arbitration. The legal fees that Claimant billed Respondents conferred exceptional value for the professional services rendered. Respondent proferred no competent evidence, by expert testimony or otherwise, to substantiate their legal malpractice and breach of fiduciary duties claims. Accordingly, fairness, equity and good conscience dictate that Respondents' breach of fiduciary duty and related malpractice claims be denied. This Award is in full adjudication of all claims and counterclaims submitted to this arbitration. All claims not expressly granted herein are hereby denied.

During this process, the arbitrator was kind enough to provide me with his wisdom of how the world of justice works. The Arbitrator said to me:

Does a physician have to be perfect? No. The law doesn't require perfection. The law only requires the professional to comply with the standard—the legal standard that other members of that profession in good standing comply with. It doesn't mean that a professional has to be absolutely perfect.

Doctors make mistakes all the time, but whether or not they complied with the legal standard, whether or not they have been professionally negligent is a question that really an expert has to address. And in court, you couldn't even offer your opinions on that would be legally irrelevant.

Now, in arbitration, we have a little different standard for relevance and so forth, but arbitrators are very inclined to give little weight to lay testimony, lay opinions when the law says we need expert opinions on that. So I say that to make this point.

How does that explanation grab you? Is this a whole pocket of horse crap? In that wonderful description of just how doctors and lawyers think the public should hold them responsible and liable for their actions, how does a layperson ever figure out a mistake was ever made if your claim just can't be weighed? Where is it written or where is it even spoken about the good standing legal standard doctors and lawyers are complying with, such that citizens can review and educate themselves on these standards? For all we know, according to this definition, for doctors, the legal standard might be if only 15 out of every 100 patients die as a result of their lack of professional care. This might well meet the legal standard that all other doctors in good standing are in compliance with, so this level of negligence is lawfully acceptable. No doctor or lawyer is expected to be perfect, and, in fact, far from it, according to Mr. Coleman, because "doctors make mistakes all the time."

How about this? What if I'm a commercial pilot and I tell you I make mistakes all the time? It's a standard in the industry among pilots who just haven't crashed yet. Want to come flying with me anytime? Come on attorneys; come flying with me!

What's the difference between a shame and a pity?

If a busload of lawyers goes over a cliff, and there are no survivors, that's known as a pity.

If there were any empty seats, that's a shame.

Can I make just one personal observation here? If *Webster's Dictionary* lists a "professional" as "one who is exceptionally skilled in some activity" and yet, attorneys practice law (I certainly do believe they consider themselves professional), then isn't it one of the best cases of a societal oxymoron in existence if attorneys want to be called professionals and simultaneously want to be associated with being respected and being known for being "exceptionally skilled," yet this arbitrator boldly claims mistakes are made all the time?

Try making that claim to iceskating judges that iceskating really doesn't require perfection. So on that note, as a pilot, I guess I could say any landing you can walk away from is considered a good one then. Is there even a slight degree of contradiction here, or is it just me? Are we to a slight degree gullible to accept this "standard"? Try this approach in any industry and see how far you get!

So, folks, just who is it that sets these standards? Does anybody know? How do they get established? Who approves of these standards—does anybody? Society and citizens sure don't have any input to these standards, now do we? Let's see 'em lawyers! Show us the standards!

Also, by their own standards, a layperson, one who is deemed nonprofessional and inexperienced according to *Webster's Dictionary*, simply has no relevant opinions that could possibly give weight to the standard of care or negligence on behalf of any lawyer.

If this is truly the case with the judicial system, and it appears this is the case, then according to this societal group of so-called professionals, who could possibly ever be smart enough to even know when you were defrauded, a victim of negligence, a victim of malpractice, or a victim of a malicious crime, because if you're not a doctor or a lawyer, by golly, you are just not smart enough to know you got taken, period!

And if that is the case, how do cases of malpractice, deceit, negligence, fraud, and so on ever get initiated because the average and ordinary person is deemed so stupid by lawyer standards that "laypeople" couldn't possibly ever recognize they were taken advantage of, let alone by perverse, unethical lawyers and attorneys. Do you take a slight offense to this attorney mentality?

Moreover, how can the average layperson ever participate as a juror and be expected to "weigh" evidence if you can never be allowed or trusted to submit evidence in a case like this? Yes sir. It takes another one of them there so-called "experts" to determine if one of them faltered according to the "you don't have to be perfect judicial/arbitration system" of fraternity brothers. And if I'm considered a layman, I should just as well write and talk like one, eh?

Do you suppose this is why you never hear about an attorney being sued or prosecuted for fraud, malpractice, negligence, or making mistakes regularly, etc., because no one knows what the pitiful legal standard is for the profession? Is this why the public is so tolerant of attorneys—because we really have no real expectations as to what we should expect from an attorney while being represented according to the laws of the land? I remind you this is coming from one of the "new arbitrator trainers for the American Arbitration Association for the last ten years" saying all this.

I truly believe the arbitrator's words to be valid to accurately dispel our current system, and it all seems to be the case. This really is the way it is. I believe the arbitrator was telling the truth as to his knowledge of how the system works and what the expectations are.

But let's take this mentality and mindset and let's see how well it would work in many ordinary layperson kinds of jobs. How safe would you feel the next time you cross a bridge if you learned earlier in the day that the engineers who designed the bridge are not perfect and they make mistakes all the time? How about the contractors who actually built the bridge? What if they weren't expected to be perfect and screwed up and left out some rebar in the concrete structure or left out some joint bolts in just one critical joint? Oh, somebody would get sued, wouldn't they?

How would you feel about a schoolteacher who isn't expected to be perfect in grading students' tests, or a firefighter who by mistake leaves trapped people behind on the way out of a house fire? How would you feel about an auto mechanic who screws up and forgets to tighten down a steering rod when replacing a power steering rack and pinion, or simply lug nuts on a wheel?

How do you feel about a billing agent or a clerk who incorrectly bills your credit card for an additional decimal point by a simple key-stroke mistake? Take a commercial pilot and let him make the mistake of incorrectly switching frequencies while talking to Air Traffic Control on an approach into Washington, DC, and see what happens. I heard this actually happened during the month of January 2011, and the Senate, which was in session, emptied the floor because they were fearful of another terrorist attack.

So, is there a mutual level of acceptance of mistakes between attorneys and laypeople who actually do something each and every day which directly affects the productivity of society? I can't screw up but you attorneys can? Hopefully I've made my point.

We have a dual standard when it comes to the legal system. I'd call the newly evolved era of our judicial system carefully coordinated, pitifully orchestrated, laced with falsification and deception, internally mocked as imperviously impenetrable, impermeable and invincible, as it applies to prosecution of attorneys. However, I do thank the system for its one saving grace—its court-recorded transcripts even though they're not perfect. I believe in this case, they did, in fact, do their job. Exposure of foul play by the juggernauts ought to truly be fair and impartial, wouldn't you think? That's about the only justice I'm going to get . . . public exposure justice of the truth of it all.

● ● ●

As the hearing progressed, Mr. Quinn evaded conviction as well as any and all disciplinary actions that should have followed by the State Bar, eluded my $940,000 counterclaim against him, and Mr. Coleman whimsically instead granted Mr. Quinn a fanciful windfall award against me.

On January 15, 2008, 4:01 p.m., Mr. DeCicco sent an e-mail to the arbitration case manager and cc'd me with comments: "With regard to Mr. Schuelke's request that there be a 'set back' (sic) of the $66,500 dollar value of the 1,250,000 share certificate which Mr. Quinn held in his possession, Mr. Quinn has three points" (set back means applied to Mr. Quinn's bill).

I'd like to share the e-mail statement referring to DeCicco's argument of justice: "The stock certificate that Mr. Schuelke references was considered with thereto and the arbitrator apparently found that its value, if any, was not relevant to the amount of the award." In other words, even though Mr. Quinn had my asset, a stock certificate which was worth $66,500 in his possession for years and it dropped in value, it is above reason to think an attorney should know what to do with its value rather than just sit and watch it go to zero . . . then give it back and claim he needs to be paid in full with interest. Isn't that another example of attorney incompetence, intent, and ineptness? Attorneys want liens applied to your recovery from a lawsuit, then once they get it, they sit on it and don't do anything with it even when it has recognized value and yet it is totally, 100% ignored in calculating the math of the final decision of this matter by the arbitrator Mr. Coleman.

There's certainly no scruples here demonstrated with respect for a client's assets while in an attorney's possession and Mr. DeCicco obviously doesn't have a problem with it either.

I thought, *OK idiot, how could you have missed this in the clear discussions about this significant value in Mr. Quinn's possession that was supposed to be mine?* I personally filed a request for reconsideration of Mr. Coleman's so-called decision and awaited a reply.

DUE DILLIGENCE

A busload of attorneys were driving down a country road when all of a sudden, the bus ran off the road and crashed into a tree in an old farmer's field. The old farmer went over to investigate. He then proceeded to dig a hole and bury the attorneys.

A few days later, the local sheriff came out, saw the crashed bus, and then asked the old farmer, "Were they all dead?"

The old farmer replied, "Well, some of them said they weren't, but you know how them attorneys lie."

CHAPTER 7:

ARBITRATION RECONSIDERATION

UPON RECEIVING THE ARBITRATOR'S decision in writing and getting over the initial shock of such a lopsided award to Mr. Quinn, I drafted and sent a letter requesting the decision to be withdrawn. I cited in my letter that Mr. Coleman violated the "Ethics Standards for Neutral Arbitrators in Contractual Arbitration." Item #13, which I cited, states clearly: "an arbitrator must ensure the party appearing without counsel has an adequate opportunity to be heard and involved," and #1 states, "They are intended to guide the conduct of arbitrators, to inform and protect participants in arbitration, and to promote public confidence in the arbitration process."

I pointed out Mr. Coleman's blatant refusal to consider any evidence without the representation of counsel and an expert clearly violated the rules of court. I also pointed out Mr. Coleman erred by not considering a set off of the $66,500 dollar value of the 1,250,000 share certificate which Mr.

Quinn held in his possession and did not apply one penny to his attorney fees. I stated, "no one should have to pay twice for fees or services."

My application, as Mr. Coleman called it, was denied. Mr. Coleman stated, "No just cause exists for modification in that Applicant was afforded a full and fair opportunity to present his claims and defenses in the underlying arbitration, in complete accord with the Association's governing Commercial Rules, the Arbitrator's Code of Ethics, and the Arbitrator's Oath of Office. The Arbitrator finds, and the record of hearing demonstrates, that the matters alleged in the application are devoid of any legal or factual basis whatsoever."

Nothing was mentioned regarding the set off of the value of the shares.

Mr. Coleman also pointed out that he himself, in fact, "announced to both parties at the first preliminary hearing and thereafter, Applicant could in fact elect for self-representation in this arbitration, pursuant to Commercial Rule R-24. And the Arbitrator announced that evidence otherwise deemed inadmissible in formal litigation, e.g., lay opinions where expert testimony is required, would be generally admitted in arbitration . . . ." But were they really?

Then Mr. Coleman made one justifiable reason for his decision that made me want to yell. Mr. Coleman states my contentions of being misled or misinformed by him of moving forward without an entourage of attorneys was "wholly unfounded."

To sum up my actions in even making an attempt to prosecute Mr. Quinn for his actions, Mr. Coleman declared, "Applicant's election to proceed without legal counsel or an expert witness was misguided."

Really, to this day I have only one main question regarding this ruling justification: Where is there justice in clearly announcing evidence is generally admitted then denied all under one breath?

How do you do that? Just because it was like Mr. Coleman announced earlier, "because I have the power"? Chew on this statement, "Nonetheless, the Arbitrator's Code of Ethics, of necessity, precludes the Arbitrator from rendering legal advice to either party," but yet he is responsible "to inform and protect participants." Is it a selective choice he can make?

Since when is it illegal to discuss the law with parties in litigation? Why should a judge or arbitrator not be able to render legal advice or the truth of law to attorneys or applicants about the laws governing the land so everyone involved can be assured they are doing what is right? What would our world be like if all police officers were that way, if we asked a question, to be told they just can't answer it? How is it that police officers are supposed to know the laws and apply them on the spot and attorneys and judges don't? I guess you police officers just got one up on the attorneys and judges, eh? You all deserve it!

Why do you suppose doctors of all various types of specialties, who equally profess to be professional, give advice to patients, but arbitrators and judges can't give advice to others as well? Why is that? Are they above the law? Or is it that they just don't know the law and they don't want anybody to know it and that might be embarrassing? They don't want to be liable for giving false or misleading statements when representing the law, even though they charge like they know everything about the law and are supposed to be representing the judicial system.

*Isn't it a shame how 99% of the lawyers give the whole profession a
bad name?*

So, we can review our classroom lecture for the day and claim we have
learned that within the judicial system and the Code of Ethics that legal
advice cannot be given to either party, correct? We need to keep legal
advice as a mystery and secret from the public so we can paradoxically
manipulate the law or laws as attorneys and lawyers so choose, or so it
appears to be to me.

For tomorrow's assignment class, go home, research, and write down how
many other professions, trades, or jobs you can think of in America that the
individual is paid for what they do and are equally not required or expected,
like judges, arbitrators, and attorneys, to give advice as to their knowledge
in their field of business. We can discuss their respective general hourly
rates tomorrow also. Class dismissed.

STATE COURT APPEAL

So there I was. I'd lost every claim against Mr. Quinn at arbitration after
spending countless hours of preparation and considerable money. And the
worst thing was I felt as though I was railroaded in the process. If, just
if, I felt I had been fairly beaten, I would have been ready to throw in the
towel and concede. But being whipped badly and having to deal with the
ruling that your case didn't have merit; that wasn't the case in my mind.
I got on the phone and started dialing every entity I could find associated
with the judicial system to search for possible options. Finally, within about

one month, I found a retired attorney who recommended me to a female attorney who might be able to help. Her name was Kathrine Winn.

Ms. Winn communicated to me via an e-mail on February 6, 2008, and stated:

> Generally an arbitrator's decision cannot be vacated or appealed due to mistakes in applying the law or for making the "wrong" decision. An arbitrator's award can be set aside if you can show misconduct which substantially prejudiced you. In your case, if the arbitrator did in fact provide legal advice to you prior to the arbitration—telling you that you did not need an attorney and that you did not need an expert witness, I believe that misconduct could be shown and you would be able to have the award vacated.

I thought, boy, was that explanation ever without logic. You can't appeal a bad decision but you can set aside one for misconduct! What gives? Why should there be any difference?

She went on to state,

> The most concerning thing that I saw with regards to the settlement was the purported representation from the settling defendants that there would be 2 million dollars put into the company to put it back into business. It seems that it would have been prudent to put on record, together with the general terms of the settlement, which you were relying upon this representation in agreeing to the settlement.

Yes, Ms. Winn. You were correct, too! I told her she needed to have been at trial to see why it was that Mr. Quinn and the defense attorney didn't put the settlement terms on record, because it left Mr. Quinn an out, and eliminated immediate grounds for filing a malpractice lawsuit against him.

(Which, by the way, is against Rule of Conduct 3-400 (B): An Attorney cannot settle a lawsuit to avoid malpractice). My complaint to the State Bar on this subject fell on deaf ears!

Ms. Winn also stated, "It seems that the value of the stock Mr. Quinn received should have been applied to your bill." Do you think? Even a simple little layman like me thought that, too! So why didn't Mr. Quinn apply the value to his bill?

I point blank asked Mr. Quinn why it was that he did this and his response was summed up by him saying, "I wasn't really sure what to do with them." Because he claimed he didn't want to sell them if the market price was too low because he knew I would complain, and he didn't know if there was enough of a market to sell them if it was going to go higher . . . so he did nothing except sit on them, because he considered them his. The shares were part of the settlement with the ABC company, yet Mr. Quinn retained these shares in his possession. He claimed he had a lien on these shares.

Ms. Winn also stated regarding liens, "I saw two retainer agreements . . . one of the retainer agreements deleted the provision giving Mr. Quinn a lien against your personal property for his fees." Another attorney interpreted it just as it was written. I wonder why no other judge could concur?

One last item I'd like to replicate of Ms. Winn's assessment: "It is true that a formal order was not drafted regarding the Requests for Admissions which were admitted pursuant to the order of the court prior to trial." This is another attorney recognizing the fact that Mr. Quinn deviated from standard protocol and sandbagged my case, thus dragging me into trial for no reason other than to pad his wallet. She gave me some consolation that she agreed there had not been real justice served at the arbitration process.

On March 1, 2008, I sent Ms. Winn a check for $2,500 to file an appeal with the State Superior Court. Ms. Winn wrote an appeal and argued profusely that I was prejudiced by not being granted a continuance when I was recorded in the transcripts clearly demanding a continuance. She argued that the arbitrator committed misconduct and so on. Ms. Winn included exact arbitration transcripts that I provided her.

My effort of an appeal was for not. I lost again. My claim was denied on June 11, 2008. The presiding state court judge was Jeffery B. Barton. Judge Barton ruled that:

> Plaintiffs have not met their burden of proof that they have been substantially prejudiced by the misconduct of the neutral arbitrator within the meaning of the Code of Civil Procedure section 1286.2(a)(3). Plaintiffs have not provided a declaration, only a transcript of the arbitration hearing. There is no transcript of the telephone pre-arbitration conference.

> The transcript supports that the plaintiff may have misunderstood what the arbitrator discussed.

Really? Who supported this idea? Was it the arbitrator versus me do you suppose?

> Therefore, Plaintiffs have not met their burden to show arbitrator misconduct. Plaintiffs also argue that they were prejudiced by the arbitrator's failure to continue the hearing. However, plaintiffs have not shown how a continuance to find an expert would have resulted differently or how they have been substantially prejudiced. There still is no expert testimony or even a declaration for plaintiffs that had an expert testified, the result would have been different. As set forth during the hearing, under the AAA rules, the arbitrator was within his discretion, after a full day of testimony, to deny a continuance after he found that Quinn would be substantially prejudiced

if it was granted. Thus, plaintiffs' motion to vacate is denied. Defendant's motion to confirm the arbitration award is granted. Interest shall accrue on the award from December 7, 2007. The court denies request for sanctions under Code of Civil Procedure section 128.7. Jeffery B. Barton – Judge of the Superior Court.

I'm just surprised he didn't grant sanctions upon me for daring to challenge an attorney! I mean after all, Quinn's attorney obviously asked the court to fine me in addition, too, but for some unknown reason, the judge denied the fine. Do you suppose I just misunderstood that, too?

Interestingly, when I first contacted Ms. Winn about this mess, she did provide some opinions after she reviewed some of my case information. After all, I believe attorneys can recognize when an American citizen gets screwed and then has to play somewhat of a sympathy card to show some moral integrity.

"Settlement of securities litigation." Ms. Winn said, "It seems that it would have been prudent to put on the record, together with the general terms of the settlement, which you were relying upon this representation in agreeing to the settlement." How can one attorney see this and yet an arbitrator can't?

"Signing over stock to Darren Quinn. It seems that the value of the stock that Mr. Quinn received should have been applied to your bill at the value that was attached to it at the time that you gave it to him." Here is yet another concept of common sense that Ms. Winn easily saw, too!

"Arbitration of malpractice claim. You will need an expert witness in order to present your claim for negligence." Ms. Winn recognizes this necessity but makes no conscious effort to line up an expert witness to back this up when she files my appeal. She ignored the essentiality of moving my case forward with the way California likes to play games. I wonder why. Do you suppose she knew full well my case wouldn't carry merit with appeals courts without expert testimony or a signed declaration, a statement of fact from another attorney?

Ok, let's review: There were no transcripts of what was said at the prehearing so we can't determine if the arbitrator did, in fact, commit misconduct. It was in the arbitration award decision that he wrote and admitted he told me such. Now, how did the judge happen to miss that? Selective reading, by chance?

Why didn't Ms. Winn include a signed declaration of statement from me? Was it another example of incompetence or do you suppose she really didn't want Mr. Quinn, a fellow attorney, to have too much evidence against him?

The judge made clear that the arbitrator felt the attorney, who was on the block for serious fraud charges, would have been prejudiced, *substantially*, if the arbitrator had granted an continuance that would have or possibly given me a fair chance to present my evidence against Mr. Quinn. It's OK to prejudice citizens, but let's not prejudice an attorney!

Ms. Winn stated, "Unfortunately, there is no further action that you can take with regards to Mr. Quinn." By now, you'd understand why I asked, "and why is that?"

Well, you see, I came to learn that Ms. Winn did have personal contact with Mr. Quinn on a previous occasion in which Mr. Quinn and Ms. Winn had worked together on a case. They both worked in the San Diego area. So I confronted Ms. Winn about this and she told me that there was no "Conflict of Interest" as to this result. If this doesn't bother you, maybe this will: I obtained a copy of the documents Ms. Winn placed with the court with my appeal, and the courts call it "lodging" your evidence with the court. Would you believe Ms. Winn did not lodge my three-ring binder of evidence with the filing of my appeal? Now, can anyone guess why?

I kept asking myself, *Why am I losing? What is wrong here? Why is it that my evidence keeps finding a way to be discharged and denied against Mr. Quinn?* The reasoning to me seemed to be so fundamentally unconstitutional, absurd, and without logic. I thought that's what the judicial system was for . . . justice, not circumventing justice!

On June 19, 2008, Ms. Winn sent me a letter stating, "If you do not file a Notice of Appeal on or before August 18, 2008, you will lose any possible right you may have to appeal."

On August 15, 2008, Ms. Winn advised in an e-mail, "I also believe that it is likely that the appellate court could award sanctions against you." This is in reference if I filed a frivolous appeal with the appellate court. Why would she have told me that? I believe she knew she had set me up for a judicial miscarriage of justice and she was threatening me not to even try prosecuting Mr. Quinn any further because she made sure my evidence never would see the light of day in a court room and could never be used against Mr. Quinn.

Regarding the conflict of interest:

The ABA Model Rules require that the client consent of attorney representation occur after full disclosure and consultation. The client must be able to appreciate the situation and have enough information to make a reasonable decision as to whether or not the legal counsel can provide fair representation. The consent of the client must also be entirely voluntary and not given under any pressure at all, by the attorney or anyone else.

Successive representation is another area where attorneys need to be careful in not having a conflict of interest. What this involves is an attorney representing a client in a matter which may be adverse to that of a former client. Since there are many more attorneys and more options for most people, this issue is arising more frequently. An attorney can be disqualified for such conduct if the interests of the former and current client are really and truly adverse in nature and if the past and current matters are closely related in some way. An attorney in such a position would risk breaching confidentiality to represent the successive client (www.essortment.com "What is the definition of conflict of interest").

Ms. Winn told me there would be no problem with her representing me against Quinn. I guess this depends which side of the fence you're on!

APPEALS COURT

After losing the State Court appeal, I was looking for a means to settle the matter with Quinn. I started calling more contacts I found on the internet to find someone who might assist in a financial settlement. I found a Forensic Accountant by the name of Jeffery Porter. He was quite entertaining to speak with. He told me he knew the best negotiator in all of San Diego, and he knew that's what I wanted. Mr. Porter gave me the name of Mr. Greg Goonan. After brief discussions regarding the mess I was in, I agreed to send both Mr. Porter and Mr. Goonan a copy of my three-ring binder of evidence against Mr. Quinn.

Mr. Goonan, after reviewing the binder, told me that my situation was so bad, he felt not only an ethical obligation to help me, but a moral obligation since the matter had been so unjustly escalated to this point.

Once I lost the arbitration hearing, Mr. Quinn was free to "confirm" the award with the state court, which would then become a collectable judgment against me. Ms. Winn attended the confirmation hearing only to bear witness and aid Mr. Quinn in the confirmation of this judgment. This is when Ms. Winn told me that "unfortunately there was nothing more I could do," which was actually a bold-faced lie. She was incorrect.

Once a judgment is entered in a state court, it doesn't become fully executable until another sixty days or so. So Mr. Quinn had to wait for this time to pass before he could start harassing me for collection. In the interim timeframe, I contacted a local attorney, Mr. Lewis Oliver, and informed him of the crap that was going on in another state and what was going to be coming here. I ran it past him and he had a few ideas. Mr. Oliver thought of the idea of filing a motion to stay the enforcement of the judgment so we could monkey more with Mr. Quinn in California with an appeal. Now, that's one attorney knowing how to mess with another one alright, so I thought.

Great. I thought that's what I really needed, another appeal. Mr. Oliver and Mr. Goonan communicated with each other, and sure enough, they convinced me to file an appeal. Mr. Goonan was initially instructed to settle the mess ASAP so we could put this nightmare behind us, or at least that's what I was led to believe.

Well, Mr. Goonan needed $10,000 upfront to review the case with an appeal specialist in Orange County and determine if we could argue a basis to settle. This sounded unwarmingly reasonable to me, but it was a plan, and as long as he could successfully negotiate a settlement for less than that amount, I was good with that. That's what I expected.

Mr. Goonan communicated back to me that the Orange County appeal specialist said it couldn't be done, but Mr. Goonan himself had a different opinion. Mr. Goonan wanted to give it a swing and attempt to pin Mr. Quinn by writing a convincing appeal.

The attorney billing invoices came pilling in and in whopping numbers. This guy charged like he believed money grew on trees.

One thing Mr. Goonan did tell me was that in his opinion, if Mr. Quinn had worked anywhere near as hard on my underlying case as he and Mr. DeCicco have in defending himself, we wouldn't be here today. That's something I could totally agree with!

In the end of the appeal, Mr. Goonan obtained an unfavorable decision from the Appellate Court since my evidence was not properly preserved at the trial court level thanks due and part to Ms. Winn for not lodging my evidence with the court. Nor did Ms. Winn provide even a declaration or expert witness testimony regarding material not considered by the arbitrator. The Appellate Court justified its decision by stating, "We conclude this claim is forfeited because of the lack of record support for it." Now that speaks volumes for the quality of legal representation.

He who says, "Talk is cheap," has never hired a lawyer.

You be the judge as to why Mr. Goonan even took such a case with the evidence unavailable in this case. However, Mr. Goonan claimed he busted his ass for me and because of his persistence, hard work and creativity, I also got out from under the contempt citation and got a stay of almost a year to respond to the judgment collection discovery. He also defeated Mr. Quinn's attempts to execute the liens on my retirement account.

Now I'd call that a monumental mound of financial betterment accomplishment in the grand scheme of things. For a guy that came with highest remarks for being known for settlement negotiation skills and not negotiating one penny of nearly $60,000 worth his attorneys' fees, he ends his report with: "So good luck in your settlement discussions with him," meaning Mr. Quinn.

So nearly $60,000 in attorneys' fees, an additional year of interest to accrue on the arbitration judgment, and he ends up negotiating nothing. Now I'd call Mr. Goonan a guy that indeed busts his ass. For what, I just can't say.

That was as far as an American citizen could go using the so-called court system in the civil courts. Nothing more could be done.

STATE BAR COMPLAINTS

My only other options were with the State Bar. Of course, I had filed the complaint with the State Bar to force Mr. Quinn to relinquish to me my files and I filed multiple complaints with the State Bar over the same course of time as during the arbitration and appeal processes.

The State Bar complaint I filed in January of 2007 was answered. The Bar informed me that the State Bar provided a notice to Mr. Quinn and that Mr. Quinn was "advised" to contact me with in ten working days of this letter regarding the availability of my client files. Under the Rules of Professional Conduct, the attorney is not required to mail or deliver the file to you, but the attorney must make them available for you to pick them up and cannot charge you for your own files. Well now, at least that worked. I got my files!

The State Bar complaint filed in May of 2007 was reviewed by a staff attorney for alleging delay in getting the default judgment and was found to be of "no consequence and no harm was caused by the delay. The alleged ineptness in handling your matter is mere negligence, at worst and not arising to an ethical violation." This complaint fell on deaf ears.

The State Bar complaint I filed in September of 2007 stated I claimed Mr. Quinn failed to competently perform in the civil trial causing substantial losses. I also stated Mr. Quinn had committed unethical misconduct and legal malpractice due to his negligence and ineptitude performance. This complaint was brushed off like it was merely a pesky fly.

On November 8, 2007, the complaint was summed up by stating, "There is no clear and convincing proof that he has violated either a rule of the Rules of Professional Conduct or a section of the Business and Professional Code."

Having felt like I had been robbed of justice once again, I contacted my local state representative who, in turn, set up a meeting with my State Senator and two Attorney General Office Senior attorneys to review my case. Since the issue had transpired out of state, the consensus among the group of four distinguished members was that the only option was to file another State Bar complaint and summons a local attorney to assist in drafting the complaint. I already had a local attorney Lewis Oliver helping me with the fight against Mr. Quinn in collection of his judgment in my county. It seemed fitting that Mr. Oliver's senior research attorney Melody Black would review the case and draft the complaint. With the evidence accompanying the complaint, we produced a complaint totaling 66 pages.

This California State Bar complaint was filed in March of 2010, and it claimed Mr. Quinn violated the State Bar Act and/or the Rules of Professional

Conduct and asked for investigation for prosecution of his alleged conduct. It also noted the complaint alleged that Mr. Quinn failed to avoid adverse interest to me when Mr. Quinn accepted stock in the company as payment for his legal fees.

THE RESULT

On June 23, 2010, the inquiry was summed up by stating,

> After careful review and after taking into consideration of all relevant factors, the State Bar has concluded that the matter does not warrant action. Your complaint about Mr. Quinn's fees has already been adjudicated. Further, it appears that the subject stock certificate was returned to you prior to arbitration.

Yes, on August 9, 2007, months after I filed my malpractice/fraud lawsuit against him and prior to him having to testify at the hearing, Mr. Quinn finally returned the share certificate and acknowledged he did not consider the certificate to be a part of my client file when he was forced to return it. The only problem was, the stock certificate was now worthless and he knew it. Mr. Quinn wanted to be able to truthfully testify that he gave back the shares. Of course, the company performed nothing more and, in fact, they all resigned and closed the business doors.

The inquiry response continued:

> Therefore, in the exercise of our prosecutorial discretion, we are closing your complaint at this time.

> You may wish to consult with other legal counsel regarding your available civil remedies. You may contact your local or county bar association to obtain the names of attorneys to assist you in this matter.

You may seek review of this decision with the Supreme Court within 60 days of this letter.

Ah, just what I needed . . . to be steered to seeking another attorney.

The stock certificate did have value during the time of the trial, but Mr. Quinn sat on it until it had little to no value and returned it when I demanded he do something with it. Mr. Quinn wouldn't sell the certificate to leave tracks showing he managed to screw me one more time and the sale would be the documented fact of his ignorance and incompetence. I believe he is a weasel in the form as the term applies.

Upon receiving the result, Melody Black had these kind words to say in an e-mail:

> Well Dennis, we gave it a good shot! I would like to think that given the time between receipt of the complaint and their decision that we at least make them think about the matters raised. I hate that they did not address the proper fee agreement language required of members of the Bar. It appears that they focused more on the stock certificate issue. If I can assist ya'll in the future with any other legal matters which may arise, please do not hesitate to contact me. Ya'll are what I call "good folks" and I wish I had been given the opportunity to assist you sooner but obviously could not because I am not a member of the California Bar. Take care ya'll. Melody.

Melody also suggested I just put this behind me and try to get on with my life. That's just not an easy thing to do when you've lost so much. All the attorneys were paid off and in full. All the attorneys were certainly happy. But not me.

SUPREME COURT COMPLAINTS

I filed two separate complaints against Mr. Quinn with the Supreme Court of the United States. One in 2008 and one in 2010.

The first one I did myself and provided the essential background of Mr. Quinn's actions. And I received the result of their review in August of 2008:

S164246

IN THE SUPREME COURT OF CALIFORNIA

En Banc

In re the Accusation of DENNIS SCHUELKE Against an Attorney

The petition is denied.

SUPREME COURT
FILED

AUG 1 3 2008

Frederick K. Ohlrich Clerk

_____
Deputy

~~GEORGE~~
Chief Justice

Upon receipt of the State Bar review stating the issue simply had been adjudicated and after discussing the result with Melody Black, I figured I had nothing more to lose if I appealed the State Bar decision on my own to the Supreme Court for one very last attempt because this wasn't making any logical sense. Ms. Black wasn't interested in providing any additional assistance. I can't say I blamed her because we had filed a lean but good complaint the first round.

So I proceeded to generate the last complaint I knew I could make, and I threw the kitchen sink of documents at it that were all relevant to the matter. These were in addition to the original 66-page complaint, so now the total was 109 pages.

This is an event you'd better be serious about since you have to make 10 copies for the Supreme Court panel, plus three copies for one part of the State Bar at one location, and one copy for another part of the State Bar at another location. So I had to make 14 copies and send them, plus I made an additional couple of copies for myself.

I sent them out on August 13, 2010, and received a post card like I had all the others stating my complaint had been received and assigned a case number. At least it wasn't rejected immediately, so that was a good thing.

I had to do this because I had to justify I did everything I could possibly do to search for justice and I just couldn't find it, even at the highest level of justice in the United States.

Then, in September 2010, came the final result of my efforts on a very similar sheet of paper like I had already received once before stating, "The petition is denied," and with absolutely no discussion or reasoning why. All that effort for four words of justification as to why Mr. Quinn was allowed to conduct himself as he did.

Here is the final decision in regards to this matter:

SUPREME COURT

FILED

SEP 2 2 2010

Frederick K. Ohlrich Clerk

_____
Deputy

S185524

IN THE SUPREME COURT OF CALIFORNIA

En Banc

In re the Accusation of DENNIS SCHUELKE Against an Attorney.

The petition is denied.

_____
GEORGE
Chief Justice

That was the case and that is what happened in the grand scheme of it all.

In the aftermath, Mr. Quinn enjoyed his own little style of vexing me since I challenged him to the letter of the law. Even though I lost, Mr. Quinn apparently wanted to continue some unprofessional conduct and just a little more unethical misconduct on his own by using the liens he had applied earlier.

I had to write a check for just over $103,000 to Mr. Quinn to satisfy his judgment. Interestingly, my local attorney Mr. Oliver never even tried to negotiate a lesser amount either and figured the total daily interest that had accrued to the very day for the payoff amount. I got stuck with paying judgment interest to the very day I had to write a huge check to Mr. Quinn for $103,587. The original balance was somewhere in the $40,000 dollar range after the trial and before Mr. Quinn appealed and you saw the mess. The rest was gratuitous interest provided by his comrades in charge.

On March 15, 2010, I gave the check to Mr. Lewis Oliver and he hand delivered it to the local counsel who Mr. Quinn used here in Tennessee, Mr. Bruce Oldham. Interestingly, the check traveled nearly 2,000 miles and was signed and deposited by Mr. Quinn in just two days. March 17, 2010 to be exact. You never have seen a group of attorneys perform better than monitoring their performance depositing your money in their accounts!

Conversely, Mr. Oliver drafted a letter and it accompanied the delivery of the check to Mr. Oldham. The letter clearly stated the matter is paid in full and the release of liens on any and all properties is demanded to be released immediately.

Would you be surprised to learn, Mr. Quinn would not and did not remove his liens? Shocking.

On June 22, 2010, at my request (because no attorney involved would do this on his own accord), Mr. Oliver drafted another letter with the same demand and sent it to the defense comrades. I had stopped by Mr. Oliver's office on several occasions to express my discontent with him and how he was handling my case, or a lack thereof actually, and demanded he get off his duff and apply the laws protecting me for once. Honoring my request as a good gesture of faith, Louis called his buddy Mr. Bruce Oldham while I was standing in Louis's office, and asked Mr. Oldham and Mr. Quinn to release the liens . . . as a courtesy call. Wasn't that nice?

Months passed and to no surprise, both Mr. Oldham and Mr. Quinn ignored the requests and violated the release of lien law provisions as provided by state law. Mr. Oliver ignored it, too. Mr. Oliver must have thought this was just another attorney joke in the making, I guess.

Finally on December 1, 2010, Mr. Quinn and Mr. Oldham removed the liens from my property.

I provided Mr. Oliver a nice two-page letter expressing my candor in wondering whose interests he was and had been representing. I asked him if he was going to file a lawsuit against Mr. Quinn for breaking the law or not. He did not and would not. This was a clear indication to me on whose interests Mr. Oliver was representing and protecting. He was charging me and I certainly believe he was accommodating Mr. Quinn. Mr. Oliver would not, in fact, file this lawsuit for me when I asked him to do so.

To me it's one thing to be stubborn, but it's far another to be downright unethical and turn your back to justice in the wake of this mess. Mr. Oliver and his associate Melody Black knew the brunt of this entire miscarriage of justice.

You thought it was over and I was done? Wrong. I couldn't help but initiate yet another lawsuit against Mr. Quinn for violating the laws of the land and for payment provided by law.

Mr. Lewis Oliver wasn't interested in filing the lawsuit against Mr. Quinn when he was my legal counsel and knew better than anyone what Mr. Quinn had done. When it came to serving up justice to another fellow attorney comrade, Mr. Lewis Oliver announced he was too busy to handle the release of lien violation and was not interested in helping me any further with legal representation. Mr. Oliver was eager to file a stay of judgment collection for me while knowing the interest accrued on the judgment, but never asked for the interest to be halted during the appeal process, and bowed out when it came time to serve justice against a fellow attorney.

So as the education comes to a close, I'd just like to incorporate the fact that the law in my state provides a maximum of a $100 fine if the liens are not removed after 45 days of receipt of the first letter. If a second letter is sent and the liens are not removed after an additional 30 days, the fine then becomes a maximum of $1,000 in addition to the $100. This fine is fixed and regulated by law, regardless of how much the amount of the lien is. On sizable matters such as mine, these figures don't amount to a mole on the south end of progress and leave the victim with not much more legal weight than a three-pound attorney resting in an urn.

I'm confident Mr. Quinn was chuckling over the release of the lien issue, since the interest which accrued on his bill was a nice little award for him in comparison to the fine imposed in my state. He likely figured it was worth it to provide just one last jab of his own.

But this time, he wouldn't be left laughing.

• • •

Finally in February of 2011, I contacted another young and aspiring quality attorney by the name of Ben Perry and I supplied him the same paperwork Mr. Oliver had. Mr. Perry jumped right on the matter and served Mr. Quinn with a lawsuit outlining Mr. Quinn's breaking of the law.

Interestingly, on May 9, 2011, Mr. Quinn's local counsel, Mr. Oldham, wrote the most dubious letter an attorney could write explaining that the demand letters Mr. Oliver wrote weren't specific enough about which liens were to be removed and that Mr. Quinn's efforts to release the liens on a timely basis were hindered because "Unfortunately, the original release apparently got lost in the mail. I assumed that Mr. Quinn had sent it to the Registers Office to be recorded. I heard nothing further until late November 2010 when Louis Oliver contacted me again." Also, Mr. Oldham stated, "We think that the proof will show Mr. Quinn did not arbitrarily and unreasonably refuse to sign a release."

How's that for a responsible judicial representative to uphold the oath of his profession and follow up on the release of the lien per the law?

On May 10, 2011, Mr. Perry followed up with a letter to Mr. Oldham indicating that Mr. Oldham would likely be called as a material witness in this lawsuit and be called to testify as to his knowledge of the matter and that he would not be allowed to represent Mr. Quinn at trial. On May 11, 2011, Mr. Oldham sent a letter that he had withdrawn from representing Mr. Quinn as his counsel and that Mr. Quinn was considering our settlement offer.

Mr. Quinn did what attorneys do and proposed a settlement agreement, which stated, "Quinn denies any failure on his part to release any judgment lien."

Additionally, Mr. Quinn wanted a Confidentiality clause, too, which stated, "Neither Party may refer to any of the terms of this Agreement unless in connection with a breach of this Agreement. The Parties may not directly or indirectly disclose the terms of this Agreement in any manner, except to their attorneys and accountants, as reasonably necessary, if such persons agree to be bound by the terms of confidentiality set forth in this paragraph. The Schuelkes agree not to refer to Darren J. Quinn, either directly or indirectly, to anyone except his attorneys."

Needless to say, I told Mr. Perry if that's what it was going to take, me signing this bucket of horse dung, then please move forward with scheduling the hearing and subpoena Mr. Quinn in front of our local judge to explain why it was that I needed to keep my mouth shut when Mr. Quinn broke the law and refused to release his liens against my properties.

It took all of about 8 minutes for Mr. Perry to call Mr. Quinn and convey my desire to go to trial against him when Mr. Perry called me right back and advised me Mr. Quinn would like to settle this matter according to our terms and would like to write a check today. Mr. Quinn took his time sending the check for $4,256.68 to cover Mr. Perry's fees and the $1,100 fine due me, but it did come.

So if you're keeping up with dates, it took two days to cash a check versus 454 days to bring closure to the release of an attorney applied lien violation!

You can see how an attorney will wiggle, squirm, deny, and attempt to cover up and conceal evidence of their unlawful doings until you prove they are acting above the law, and caught.

Yes, it might take time, but it does go to show you can stand your ground against an attorney and win when you play their game long enough. It takes some doing to find a quality attorney like Ben Perry who will actually honor his oath to uphold the law, but the system can work if you have your ducks in a row, have the knowledge of the law, and the gall to take it to them.

• • •

If this is the standard, how bad does it have to get before Americans wake up from the hypnotic state of nirvana? Will it take a new world American Gestapo type of Federal agents to show up unexpectedly at your door step to wisp your naïve carcass off to jail for being caught using illegal incandescent light bulbs or for not showing your papers that you are buying government health care?

How many other Americans need to experience the same crap before we get into gear and start judicial reform, similar to the response and energy given to little two-year-old Caylee Anthony and Caylee's Law?

While I was encouraged by the response America gave to the senseless death of this child—it certainly shows America does and can pay attention to injustice—I've yet to see America respond to the corruption in the judicial system.

What do you have when a lawyer is buried up to his neck in sand?

Not enough sand.

CHAPTER 8:

TRICKUM BACK

IN MY OPINION, if there ever was an area of practiced law that an attorney will never tell you about—dragging you unjustly into and through the cesspool of judicial mud is one of them, and here is why I believe so. Attorneys have no scruples even if you are victimized and they rub your noses in it to accentuate the matter even more! I don't believe it has to be this way. Through this whole ordeal, I gained some valuable lessons learned. If you are ever faced with having to go to a civil trial against someone who you know is lying and you are the plaintiff, think about these points for what it is worth. (This is civil only, not criminal.)

- You lived through the negative experience once already. You are simply making the effort for righteousness.

- Your attorney will ask you to relive the whole scenario the second time by requiring you to dig up and produce all your documentation in a chronological time-frame format. Then the opposing attorney will most likely demand hours of your time to sit for questioning for a deposition, so you relive the scenario for the third time.

- Attorneys know exposure to the courtroom is not an atmosphere most people enjoy, answering questions under oath directly in front of a judge and or a jury. So, if your attorney says he will put you on the stand as the first witness and go over everything that happened, there are four highly negative things that happen to you right off the bat:

1. You are exposed to the emotional stress of it all one more time, which most likely is going to be for the third or fourth time. This exposure is a drag on you anyway you look at it. No matter how good of job you do, you will likely wonder how you came across and you will likely wonder if you could have done better or if you missed something. You'll most always think of something else you should have said and really wanted to add but your chance is gone.

Witness testimony, especially for cross-examination is not rehearsed. If you give your testimony and step down knowing you said everything you wanted and wouldn't add a thing, you are lucky; otherwise you just helped your attorney and the defense set up the least wanted outcome you could possibly desire . . . a compromising settlement, leaving you with a half empty glass.

So the main result has just added to your stress level and your own uncertainty. You just became more tired of the mess. I believe attorneys actually like it that way. You'll soon see why I say that.

2. By you going first on the witness stand, you give the defense attorney and his clients the comfort of sitting and casting their eyes on you and they can take notes on everything you say.

This is one of the greatest disadvantages that you as a plaintiff could ever want to be faced with, because the defense will be looking to blow holes in your testimony. If you give testimony first, you open yourself up to be cross-examined first also. You are now fair game to questioning over everything you said. The focal light has been placed on you, not the defendant who is the guilty one! This is not what you want and is not the way to start out your case!

3. You lose the opportunity for everyone present to view the defendant first who is the one charged with the incident.

You will not have the same opportunity to question the defense's smaller and more specific volume of testimony because you are the one who has to walk through the entire case. The defendant will have a far smaller task in his defense than you. You just set yourself up for a higher chance of failure. Actually, your attorney just set you up for this higher chance of failure. This is why your attorney will tell you only one beneficial piece of advice during your testimony on the witness stand: answer every question with short answers and do not ramble. Why? That ought to be self-explanatory; you set yourself up to be questioned further on cross-examination for no good purpose.

Ask yourself this question: at trial, which are people going to be more concerned about; what you did right or what the defendant did wrong? If you have a good case, put it on first against the defendant. Sling the mud and if it sticks, it will stay in place, assuming your attorney can do a good job. If your attorney is incompetent you'll at least know it from the start and know you may have to take a compromising settlement.

After all, as I have displayed in this book, my attorney obtained evidence in my case against the defendant and told me he could nail the defendant for fraud, only to find out the evidence was not admissible because he obtained the evidence illegally. Had Mr. Quinn simply obtained this evidence legally, my case certainly would have had a dramatically different outcome. So, you need to know these things up front in your trial, not after you have been put on the stand, because it makes you look like you are a jerk just like your attorney! You both lose credibility in front of the judge and jury when this happens.

If your attorney won't take your case on a contingency fee basis instead of an hourly one, then they expect to get paid even when they screw up, regardless of how bad! So, why should they care?

4. And last, but certainly what should not be the least of concern, is the competence of your attorney.

For heaven sake, don't be naïve to think that your attorney is perfect and won't make mistakes. You have seen what Mr. Quinn did in my trial. Your attorney could likely also perform so incompetently that both the judge and the defense attorney have to assist and suggest to your own attorney how to ask questions to establish what is referred to as foundation or relevance to the question being asked. This pitiful show of ignorance on several occasions, let's say, doesn't generate any strengths on your side as a plaintiff in the eyes of the ever-so-important jurors or judge. Or when the judge sees your attorney pull something like attempting to use illegally obtained evidence in trial, you can imagine, you've not won any brownie points. If you think you had a mulligan, you just used it.

Besides, wouldn't you rather know about the gut-wrenching deplorable capability of your attorney early on when it comes to establishing your evidence against your defendant, or should I say, incapability of presenting your evidence and thus leaving YOU looking like a schmuck who files a claim for no good reason? Why not save yourself the embarrassment and all those hours on the witness stand and all those attorney billing hours you know you're sure to get?

Attorneys will never tell you these details of trial. Why? Because a high percentage of trials settle and never go all the way through a full entire trial and require the judge and or jury to render their verdict. Your attorney is doing you a disservice making you give your testimony first if you are the plaintiff. Never let an attorney do this to you! I'm convinced it is a proven part of the game they play, and I do mean play, with you, your money, and your case, by playing you on the witness stand, versus the real person who should be up there—the defendant!

If you allow your attorney to do this to you, you will have a far higher chance and likelihood of having to settle your case rather than prevail. If the attorneys can prevail in driving you to a compromised settlement, neither attorney takes the crown or falls, and the clients take a compromising settlement.

Besides, I already tried it and you've seen how it is that I got Mr. Quinn on the witness stand and recorded some of my questions directly to him. Tell me that it doesn't work! If I hadn't drilled Mr. Quinn in front of a court recorder first, I'd most likely have had zero testimony from Mr. Quinn to furnish to you.

Lawyers are like beavers: They get in the mainstream and damn it up.

I am dually convinced the game is set up that way and the attorneys certainly won't fill you in on the process and how it works beforehand.

You are just a money tree to them. The more they can shake you, the more money they will get out of you. Remember this, too. If you settle, just know this; your attorney will charge you to draft the settlement agreement, argue the terms, talk to you about it, charge you for it, and this goes on for many additional billing hours you will be charged for.

So, you take charge of the order of *your* trial and tell your attorney to put the defendant up first. Demand that your attorney confirm all the background events leading up to your disagreement, with the defendant, which takes time. There is absolutely no good reason for you to have to do this. Wear down and embarrass the defense first with your evidence rather than you being questioned on your integrity first, because that is what will happen.

Plus, if your attorney does not have all your evidence prepared for you to utilize to defend yourself, you just disadvantaged yourself in trial. I'm speaking from experience. Your attorney is not going to go out of his way to have all your evidence at your fingertips when you are on the stand.

As I understand the difference between civil and criminal trials, most of the time, the defendant takes the Fifth Amendment and never has to take the witness stand and cannot be forced to testify. This is why I would most certainly like to clarify this only applies to civil trials.

Sadly, the statistics show overwhelmingly that only one in five winning civil trial judgments collect restitution, in other words, only one in five ever see any money returned from the defendant. If there were ever a false impression associated with civil courts, this is one. That is something attorneys won't openly disclose to new clients. Why is that? Restitution just isn't a part of the game attorneys and judges in civil justice give a hoot about.

It is a fact that there aren't any teeth behind a civil judgment to force a crook to repay you a dime if you get a judgment against a crook. Attorneys love this, too. They don't and most won't attempt to do anything further for you. Mr. Quinn certainly wouldn't do a thing with the over $650,000 judgment. All he said was, I don't do collections.

Collection attorneys typically want a minimum of 33% to as much as 50% of the value of your judgment should you bear the time, costs, and headache through the civil courts to obtain one. Hopefully you don't need to be a rocket scientist to figure out your remaining share left, even if the collection attorney could collect the entire amount for you. Hopefully you can see that you are left with 25% or less by the time you pay all attorney's fees associated with civil litigation to obtain a civil judgment. I don't know how many times I've heard individuals in this country say civil judgments aren't worth the paper they're printed on. My case certainly added to bolster this fact. What a joke!

I'd recommend if you are ever in this predicament and you can't find the avenue to prosecute criminally, don't. You will save your money, your time, and skip the risk of losing it all to some attorney who couldn't care less if you win, lose, or collect one dime. That's my recommendation. Civil court judgments are just another joke in the American judicial system.

Ask the family of the murdered Ron Goldman who was awarded a civil judgment against O.J. Simpson if the American judicial system provides excellent restitution from a civil judgment. The jury panel, in this case, ordered Simpson to pay $8.5 million in compensatory damages to the Goldman family for the loss of Ronald Goldman's life. Yet, it is my understanding O. J. Simpson has never paid a portion of this verdict. What good is the judgement or the piece of paper it's printed on? Either way, no amount of money can substitute for a life.

A LAWYER AND AN ENGINEER

A lawyer and an engineer were fishing in the Caribbean when they got to talking. The lawyer mentioned, "I'm here because my house burned down and everything got destroyed by the fire. The insurance company paid for everything."

"That's quite a coincidence," remarked the engineer. "I'm here because my house and all my belongings were destroyed by a flood. My insurance company, too, paid for everything."

There was a brief pause, and then the puzzled lawyer asked, "How do you start a flood?"

CHAPTER 9:

MY CONFESSION

WAS I A GUILTY PARTY in this mess? I'd sure say I was. I was both negligent and naïve in the entire scope of what modern-day legal representation is all about. I had never experienced this level of courtroom drama before, and subsequently, my expectations were way off base. I trusted my attorney for far too long.

I signed my attorney's modified retainer agreement and Mr. Quinn signed mine without first taking them to another attorney to be sure I understood how all the provisions within the retainer agreement could fully impact me; in that I, or anyone else for that matter, really had no way of predicting future unethical administerial acts by an attorney. The problem was, and I still believe today, you won't find an attorney who will warn you of the all the potential pitfalls of another attorney's contractual clauses that are there for their protection against State Bar prosecution and the justice system and so on. Attorneys aren't going to tell you that you can get taken to the cleaners like this. If an attorney wants to bilk you, they're going to bilk you! If I were a betting man, I'd bet you won't find one in the million licensed numbers of them who would give you a truthful rendition like this of how bad it can be if you hire an attorney. Do I have any takers? After all, you have witnessed the fact that if you draft any type of agreement with your attorney and have him or her sign it, it doesn't mean anything. They only are to be mindful of it.

I was guilty of not taking heed to the fact that Mr. Quinn did not have malpractice insurance and I was not very clairvoyant in knowing just how impactful this can be when you actually feel justified in pursuing fraud charges against an attorney and just how difficult it can be finding another attorney to represent you if you intend to file fraud charges against an attorney.

I've never seen an attorney retainer contract that openly spells it out as malpractice insurance for fraud, deceit, unethical practice, malice, conversion (referring to committing untrustworthy crimes), but rather cleverly, cunningly, and tactically list what they obviously downplay the potentially huge liability against them as "errors and omissions" insurance to give the public the idea that they make only typographical or unintended errors in documents.

I was unable to foresee the reality that every attorney I spoke with out of dozens was not interested in taking my malpractice case against Mr. Quinn solely because Mr. Quinn did not carry malpractice insurance. Why? They all were afraid if they did win against Mr. Quinn that they most likely would never get paid and to those attorneys, charging Mr. Quinn was rather pointless. It wasn't about winning or serving up justice against what I believe was a crooked attorney, it was about getting paid.

I obviously faulted by not digging into Mr. Quinn's retainer agreement for further clarification and understanding of the impact and full ramifications of his "Statement of Insurance Coverage":

> We do not maintain errors and omissions insurance coverage. We have not filed with the State Bar an executed copy of a written agreement guaranteeing payment of all claims established against us by you for errors or omissions arising out of the practice of law by us in the amount specified in paragraph (c) of subsection B of Rule IV of the Law Corporation Rules of the State Bar.

Why don't attorneys just call it what it is—malpractice insurance instead of errors and omissions insurance? This is this just another little subtle form of deceit attorneys use to purposely skim over the real term of malpractice and avoid discussion on the subject of blunders. So they greatly reduce the likelihood of having to talk to you up front about who is responsible if the attorney makes a serious mistake that costs you big money, regardless of whether or not they intentionally commit an error that impacts the result of your case. You might well be thinking it just covers typographical mistakes in filings, briefs, or court documents and nothing to do with the attorney's competence, honesty, ethics, and actual performance.

I signed Mr. Quinn's retainer agreement, which by law resultantly denied me my right to one of the basic founding principles and articles of the very Constitution of the United States of America—my right to a jury trial. Mr. Quinn took full advantage of his Arbitration clause:

> Any dispute between the parties hereto arising out of or relating to this agreement or our legal services rendered to or for client shall be resolved by binding arbitration before the American Arbitration Association in San Diego, California and each side shall bear their own costs and attorney fees.

I was naïve for thinking my documented evidence against Mr. Quinn would be fairly considered and weighed in any such judicial oriented forum as in Arbitration, let alone in his own state and backyard of local judges.

I was guilty for not firing Mr. Quinn in the early months when he did not live up to his stated intentions of obtaining the cashed check which was to be the sole proof of the fraud, as he said. I allowed him to toy with my case rather than demand he stick to his original statement that if we obtain the check and the company spent the money in just a few days, the fraud would be established and a trial will never be necessary. I let him lead. I did not realize I was being played by what I perceived too late in the game to be an unethical attorney in my eyes but was clearly not an unethical attorney in the eyes of the judicial process as we have today. I was unable to foresee the avalanche of Mr. Quinn's detrimental actions and I erred by not discharging him after the multitude of administerial acts that had profound impacts to my ability to obtain actual restitution.

A man was prosecuted. The judge asked him, "Don't you need a lawyer?"

To which he replied, "No, I don't need one. I'm going to tell the truth."

I never should have listened to Mr. Quinn even in the beginning when he advised me not to take my case to the State and Federal district attorneys' office for criminal charges to be filed because he told me we would lose control of our civil case and that each and every person of the other 600 to 700 that got bilked out of the 23–25 million dollars would be in on the class action lawsuit the State or Feds would file, leaving me with little to no chance to expect restitution even though the criminals would go to jail.

This certainly was a criminal case and it should have been handled as one. Oh, do I wish I'd been able to file criminally instead of civil. Now that's Monday night armchair quarterbacking right there! Criminal prosecution, I don't believe, plays the games that the civil attorneys do. The stakes are totally different.

I confess I didn't know at the time when Mr. Quinn was sworn in at arbitration that I maybe should have demanded the arbitrator to read both Mr. Quinn and Mr. Pettit their so-called "Miranda Rights" so that their transcript testimonies could be easily used against them for criminal prosecution if lying during testimony. I didn't know that, but I do now.

Therefore, I am guilty of still believing I was wronged by Mr. Quinn and I was guilty of believing the judicial system would fundamentally provide equal rights for all. I certainly no longer believe that at all.

I believe the civil side of the judicial system could be discarded 90–95% (small claims seems to work more effectively) and just empower your local policeman to resolve issues or else empower them to take one of the parties to jail to think about it. I'd trust a policeman 10 to 1 before I'd trust another civil attorney with my case.

If somebody takes a quarter of a million dollars of your money and you don't even get a receipt, I think if you explain that to your local policeman, he wouldn't have a problem escorting you to the person, handcuffing them on the spot, and hauling them off to jail. I'm thinking this might clean up society rather quickly.

I did not understand that attorneys and lawyers are expected and allowed to make mistakes all the time. Those mistakes can impact your case and there just really aren't any standards by which a layperson can judge or gauge an attorney's performance; and certainly a layperson cannot, by any standard, provide any tribunal evidence to the contrary.

I was a fool to think I could prosecute an attorney in the Arbitration system as it is set up today. The only thing it accomplished was it generated some eye-opening and jaw dropping transcripts that I don't believe the involved parties would particularly like exposed to the public.

I have transgressed beyond the verdict of the arbitrator and exposed Mr. Quinn's administerial acts or occurrences which I still believe weren't just unethical but fraudulent. For that matter, you've had some opportunity to judge the actions of several other attorneys and judges regarding their conduct as well.

I still believe in a little simple daily oath, "Do unto others as you would have them do unto you."

Sadly and truthfully, now, when I'm in public citing the "Pledge of Allegiance" to the American flag, I can no longer finish the last words "with liberty and justice for all," because I don't believe it! I believe corruption is far too prevalent and blazingly obvious for this to be true.

The laws of the land have apparently become so parched, convoluted, and confusing to not only the average American citizen, but even to the police who also represent the law. Police officers even have difficulty differentiating between criminal and civil infractions. The inequality of crimes committed and the varying punishment standards are literally insane.

● ● ●

I have to share this vastly different result for a crime done on a miniscule level compared to Mr. Quinn and the dollars involved. It's staggeringly shocking.

To cite an example of this, in the summer of 2009, my son was searching for a car to purchase and rebuild so he could have something to drive when he turned 16. He found an older one on e-bay that he wanted and commenced to make the purchase.

It so happened that after he sent the money via a wire transfer, the listed transfer agent would not respond and within just a few hours the recipient claimed they had not received the money and claimed we were just trying to steal their car. It was approximately 7:00 p.m. on that same day, when we received an e-mail claiming we had not sent the money and so on. I told my son he had been taken.

We discussed this during dinner, ran off a copy of the e-mail, and headed to our local police department with our paperwork and described what had happened. The desk officer looked at our situation and told me we had a civil matter and that we needed to contact an attorney if we wanted any action taken. He told me that since it was a contractual type of dispute, the police could not involve themselves. I told him that just didn't sound right and left to go back home feeling really bad for my son.

You know, I just was having a hard time with the policeman's response of, "you'll have to hire an attorney," and that night I just couldn't get that out of my head. It wouldn't let me sleep.

At about 2:30 in the morning I got up, got dressed, and came up with an idea. I jumped in the car and headed to the 24-hour store where my son sent off the money transfer and found some very helpful employees.

The tracking of the funds was traced within minutes and we found where they went. It was out of state. We obtained a phone number of the store that received the funds, placed a call, and found out that only half of the money had been picked up simply because the store didn't normally keep large amounts of cash on hand.

I told them the deal was a scam and fraudulent and I asked them to call the police if the individual comes back to cash in the remainder. They said they would do just that. I also called the local police in that state and informed them of the situation. They told me to just have the store call them immediately when the individual returned and they would assist ASAP.

Right at 9:00 a.m. the same individual returned and asked to pick up the remaining cash. The attendant was well prepared and asked the individual to please be patient for a couple of minutes while they obtained the money. Meanwhile they called the police. It worked perfectly! The police were there in less than 2 minutes, walked in to where the individual was patiently waiting, and handcuffed him immediately. The police found three different IDs in his possession and the store manager said the police asked him, "so which one of these people are you?" The individual's only response was, "looks like I'm going to go to jail for a long time."

Would you believe the individual was handcuffed, taken to the local police precinct, finger printed, and charged with theft by deception and forgery 1st degree. In September of 2010, the individual was sentenced to three years in jail, ordered to pay restitution in monthly allotments when released, and will remain on parole for another three years thereafter.

Shocked yet? The amount involved was $2,000.

Now, how and why was it that my local police department turned me away and instructed me to go get an attorney, that it was a civil matter, and the officer would not even write up an incident report? Yet, another state's police department eagerly and immediately took my call and was on it like invaded bees around their beehive. How ironic is it that simply in another police precinct, the incident took on a whole new face? From what was deemed a civil matter in one police precinct requiring me to leave, go home, and spend hordes of money to hire an attorney, in the other precinct it was dramatically opposite in the attitude aiding and assisting me which took flight to a full blown "criminal" matter which takes on a totally different judicial attitude with fabulous results that not only met but exceeded my expectations! There are absolutely no standards within the judicial system today.

If it weren't for lawyers, we wouldn't need them.

What I have learned is this: If someone intentionally deceives you from the start for their benefit and you have signed a contract and you can prove the deceit, you're in much better shape attempting to bring criminal justice to perverse individuals. To the contrary, if you have a contract and you can't show the "intent" to defraud you but they just did, then you will most assuredly be mandated by the judicial system to deal with the matter in what is known as "civil" courts.

That then leaves one huge difference to you personally if you are the one on the losing end. Criminal investigation and prosecution is paid for by tax dollars, while civil cases require you to hire an attorney and flip the bill on your own. If you are the sort of person who doesn't like to keep documents, e-mails, letters, and communication notes all fairly organized for your business dealings, then you aren't likely to prevail in either forum because you have to prove your case either way. This is one time in life that it does pay to keep everything!

Another thing: charged individuals in criminal cases rarely ever take the stand at trial and never have to answer questions. Criminals usually plea the Fifth Amendment which gives them immunity so they do not have to testify. If you have a jury trial, you have to show enough proof to convince all twelve jurors by a unanimous decision of guilt, or otherwise if even one juror votes not guilty and eleven vote guilty, the charged individual walks free. It's something to think about.

Oh, I have thought about this little episode many times and compared it to my eleven years of experience with the much larger case, and the result. It strikes me staggeringly numb as to why $2,000 in a slightly different setting can land someone in jail with all the associated punishment and treatment. Yet conversely, you have witnessed the exact gross opposite experience with attorneys and the civil system with a case that was hundreds of times larger. The losses in this case were, suffice it to say with all the investment losses, attorney fees, and miscellaneous fees—a million dollars. It involved so much more importance and significance to me, but the result was unbelievably insulting. I am convinced there is absolutely no equality of justice in our American judicial system today. No one could ever possibly convince me otherwise.

Anyone could claim I became obsessed with searching for truth and just wouldn't give up. When you follow the path this judicial system took me on, I refused to believe what kept happening was fair and just! I'll confess, right or wrong, I am just too bullheaded to let the sleeping dog lie. It turns my crank to witness liars and cheats do it and get by with it. I believe our system needs to stop making cupcakes for the perpetrators and get back to doling out some common sense punishment for their crimes. If you do the crime, you should do the time—and attorneys should be no exception!

THE TRUCK DRIVER, THE PRIEST, AND THE LAWYER

A truck driver used to amuse himself by running over lawyers he saw walking down the side of the road. Every time he saw a lawyer walking along the road, he swerved to hit him and there would be a loud "THUMP." Then he would swerve back on the road.

One day, as the truck driver was driving along the road, he saw a priest hitchhiking. He thought he would do a good deed and pulled the truck over.

"Where are you going, Father?" The truck driver asked.

"I'm going to the church five miles down the road," replied the priest.

"No problem, Father! I'll give you a lift. Climb in the truck." The happy priest climbed into the passenger seat and the truck driver continued down the road. Suddenly, the truck driver saw a lawyer walking down the road.

Instinctively he swerved to hit him. At the last moment, he remembered there was a priest in the truck with him, so he swerved back to the road and narrowly missed the lawyer.

Certain he should've missed the lawyer, the truck driver was very surprised and immediately uneasy when he heard a loud "THUMP." He felt really guilty about his actions and so turned to the priest and said, "I'm really sorry Father. I almost hit that lawyer."

"That's okay," replied the priest. "I got him with the door."

CHAPTER 10:

CONCLUSION

THE EXACT DATE that professional attorneys came into existence is unknown, although the first complaints about them were recorded in the twelfth century.

In the 1970s, when the Nixon Watergate scandal transpired, the State Bar sent out a survey questionnaire wanting the public's opinion as to what the public thought about attorneys and what attorneys could do to improve their reputation. I don't believe I've personally seen any documented evidence that there has been any improvement.

You've now seen evidence of what I experienced with attorneys and the judicial system and the result(s). Yes, you could say I believe Thomas N. Carter, Joseph E. Lindquist, John Albert Cole, and Timothy J. Conner are laughing, too. This had to be a big joke screwing the public for millions of dollars and getting away with it. We won't ever know, but I believe their defending attorney, Mr. Kennan Kaeder, himself on his own reconnaissance, might well have written Mr. Quinn that $3,000 check (which I have a copy of), just to see this whole case and its slight potential maximus of the sword imperilment and embarrassment—just to go away as if it never even happened.

In the eyes of Mr. DeCicco, Mr. Pettit, Mr. Coleman, Judge Barton, Judge DiFiglia, the California State Court, The California Appellate Court, the Supreme Court of California, the California Office of the Governor, and the State Bar . . . Mr. Quinn is an icon in good standing within our judicial system, a supposed judicial watchdog branch of government. This is not a respected branch of our American government in the eyes of many . . . that I am confident in saying.

Did I prove in the courts that Mr. Quinn committed professional negligence, breach of fiduciary duty, and conversion? No, I failed. Mr. Quinn was found in our American court system to be guilty of nothing . . . absolutely nothing in California, but he sure wouldn't come back to Tennessee, where he was originally from, to try his San Diego School of Law style of judicial poker! The American judicial courts and the arbitration system upheld, embraced, embellished, and I'm guessing even gorged and relished themselves in winning and dening prosecution of this highly contested professional negligence fraud case. I believe the records show there was ample evidence of unethical conduct, malpractice, intentional deceit, oppression of evidence, violation of the Professional Rules of Conduct, which is supposed to be governed by the State Bar, even though other attorneys are paid to plan and deliver bogus testimony contrary to the facts of the case. In addition to me, who wouldn't be flabbergasted and stunned to learn the attorney himself later claimed the basis of this whole mess "didn't pass the lawyer smell test" in the beginning! Yet somehow, Mr. Quinn found justification for a $660,000 judgment against one individual and filed for 2.7 million dollars in fraudulent damages in this case. Is it just me or is it justified when an attorney fails to achieve restitution for the victim—when an attorney turns about face and pitifully claims the case wasn't worth filing in the beginning and then certainly gives no grounds to complain about professional unethical conduct and a shameful result?

I believe there was ample evidence that there are those attorneys and lawyers within our American judicial system who lie and therefore cannot be trusted and that this creates a slight problem for American citizens and American businesses . . . we don't know which attorneys or judges we can trust. The State Bar took all my complaints and I believe must have considered them all as a joke.

For that matter, I believe Katherine Winn, Gregg Goonan, Lewis Oliver, and Bruce Oldham also must have thought this case was one big joke because they all got handsomely paid in the process!

My horrible experience with this mess is over, but my fear is for the rest of you! Are you going to be the next victim of lying, mistake-prone, unethical attorneys who know prosecution is nothing but a joke on you?

Are you just a tick on the clock away from becoming another victim like these cases?

- The Ronald Goldman family as O.J. Simpson walks free;

- Another Bernie Madoff Ponzi scheme victim defrauded out of your retirement as Madoff rots in jail and you're left with no restitution;

- Another Enron/Kenneth Lay scandal where investors lost nearly $11 billion dollars and the judicial system acted, but still employees and shareholders received limited returns in lawsuits, despite losing billions in pensions and stock prices;

- Another child like Caylee Anthony dead in a grave as the prosecuting attorneys pat themselves on the back for doing a good job while only proving Casey lied to the police;

- The American public with wool pulled over its eyes as many embraced John Edwards as he ran for the president of the United States twice, now knowing he is a liar. What else has he or will he lie about as a politician?

- The American public cunningly convinced by former president Bill Clinton that he didn't have sex with Monica Lewinski in the Oval Office of the White House, even as Mr. Clinton pointed his finger into the camera making this claim. What else did he lie about as a politician?

- The American public and the Country itself flounders in government debt and irresponsible spending by a government acutely infiltrated by attorneys who couldn't care less how, where, when, and who makes money—they just want it, much more of it, and they are willing to lie/make mistakes without standards of care/fend off charges to the most perverse, regardless of the consequences to anyone or the country.

Get over the idea that attorneys can all be trusted! The next time an attorney takes the podium to give a speech, I'd suggest you consider the words to be coming out of their mouths just like it was coming out of Darren J. Quinn's or Paul M. DeCicco's or Douglas Pettit's, until the laws of this land dramatically bring up the standards for lawyers and attorneys because the laws and standards are one big joke!

Again, there is no effective system to discipline attorneys and lawyers. Attorneys have established a dual system of prosecution of justice for which they consider themselves above the law and America has let it happen. Judicial mandates of organizational integrity trust and truth are nonexistent. The liberty bell is cracked and silent, yet individuals like you and me suffer as a result of the numb, faceless, and conniving judicial justices with passive passion who sit and watch the invasion of corruption of our rights as they erode away.

If the Bible's version of Proverbs 12:22 summed up has any significance to anyone or any place in the expectation of our judicial system: "God detests lying lips, but God loves those men who tell the truth," then, it's high time the American society, the government, the State Bar, and this country wake up as a whole, review, and restart our original intentions for why there was a glorious fight for liberty for so many.

I'm over the fact that I lost one hell of a war with justice, corruption, and attorneys. Even though I won a little battle in the end that had little significance, it proved the point—there are those attorneys who consider themselves above the law and argue profusely they aren't. The question is, are you savvy enough to tell the difference in them? Take my recommendations, get off your duff, and take some action before you become a victim, too!

Just remember: When you go to court, you are trusting your fate to twelve people who weren't smart enough to get out of jury duty!

Will the complaints ever stop? Probably not. But can the system be greatly cleaned up and improved? I say it can.

I've given you an education that just isn't available anywhere in abundance, yet so many of you already knew or had an inkling that this kind of nonsense has been transpiring among us for years. Get up, work with me, and start sounding the alarm. Next, I've got some simple—and I believe extremely effective—recommendations for you as a guide.

Educate yourself before you are the next victim!

As I previously mentioned at the end of Chapter 3 "The Root of It All," I suggested familiarizing yourself with the missing original 13th Amendment to the Constitution of the United States that most certainly existed, but mystically disappeared. I must reiterate my conclusion even at the risk of appearing dogmatic until you research what our founding forefathers did, in fact, initially intend for this republic—to withstand tyranny and corruption and to prevent the judicial branch from becoming arrogantly out of control.

I've come to realize the principal intent of this "missing original 13th Amendment" was to prohibit lawyers from serving in government. To me, this would have prohibited all the underlying judicial unethical conduct which has led to the litany of self-servant laws we witness today and the unbelievable audacity of the modern culture of attorneys like Darren J. Quinn.

The missing 13th Amendment, called Article XIII, reads:

"If any citizen of the United States shall accept, claim, receive, or retain, any title of nobility or honor, or shall, without the consent of Congress, accept and retain any present, pension, office, or emolument of any kind whatever, from any emperor, king, prince, or foreign power, such person shall cease to be a citizen of the United States, and shall be incapable of holding any office of trust or profit under them, or either of them."

Its removal is no little "faux pas" and it was intentional, just like the injustice in my entire eleven-year case.

RECOMMENDATIONS

Here are my recommendations as to how to address the flaws in our current judicial system:

1. Educating yourself is the first step to recognizing that we have a serious problem—HOUSTON!

I certainly feel as an astronaut would—hung out in space with a nonfunctioning rocket booster. Except in this case, we have no one at home in politics who even cares to listen or anyone who is even talking about it! We've been hung out to dry for far too long!

The entire judicial system needs to reform the process of getting and dealing expeditiously with the truth. Liars need to suffer stiffer consequences of lying!

2. Stop voting attorneys into public offices until judicial reform transpires and until true due process of law is instituted.

This will send the quickest signal to clearly suggest American citizens will no longer tolerate dual standards of justice and continue to tolerate injustice.

My newly elected Representative and a former attorney Linda Elam will not and has not taken or returned any of my phone calls since she has taken office. This certainly is to be expected for the obvious reasons; attorneys are extremely content with the current laws and judicial systems they have put into place to regulate disciplinary actions against themselves and they themselves aren't about to touch this glorious climatic arena of dual standards. So, just probe around just a little and you will find more receptive representatives like Senator Mae Beavers who is, in fact, taking action in these areas and who can use your support.

Again, not all attorneys are thugs in my opinion, but I don't believe you should walk into an ambush once you are alerted of one either, agreed? It is my goal to inform and educate the public so hopefully no one will say something like, "I wish I would have known that."

Simply, if one person will sound the alarm on judicial corruption and tell another three people every week, we're only talking a few short months time until the majority of voters can impact the voting polls and send the clear signal as to our dissatisfaction with the current system and state of affairs.

3. Start contacting your local state representatives, senators, and congressmen and request the abolishment of the entire ineffective disciplinary system of attorneys and judges.

The entire system of disciplining judges and attorneys needs to go in the toilet.

Unethical conduct of any type and fraud charges should only be decided in front of a jury of local non-judicial comrades so the local community does, in fact, have the same opportunity to put corrupt attorneys behind bars and access fines right along with non-attorney citizens. Yes, I believe many a citizen would indeed like to sit on a jury panel to have a crack at justice served to attorneys and judges as appropriate. Maybe any and all charges and violations against attorneys, like simply traffic violations, need to be heard in the presence of the local community, such that these and all violations need to carry a stiffer penalty (or at least the normal penalty) since attorneys ought to be the precedent setters upholding the law, not setting the precedence for breaking the laws.

4. Never sign an attorney's retainer agreement which precludes you from your constitutional rights to a jury trial, should you get into any type of "dispute" with your attorney.

Do not sign away any of your rights to a jury trial. Do not agree to any form of arbitrations or so-called mediations as a mandatory resolve to potential disputes.

If you don't think there is anything to this, check with the State Bar of California and investigate their amended June 23, 2005, 31-page "Fee Agreement Form" of instructions and comments. This is regarding California's pathetic attempt to "eliminate unnecessary legalese" and to make attorneys' disclosures "complete, accurate, and not misleading." Even their guidelines "suggest" and state that it "is appropriate" that an attorney utilize binding arbitration of all claims other than fee disputes.

*Let me be very clear here—the State Bar is suggesting to all attorneys that they have you, as a client, sign away your right to the Sixth Amendment of the Constitution of the United States of America—*your Constitutional right to a jury trial of average citizens and not attorneys who can corrupt the very system you may need to rely on. So, if you have an attorney who asks you to sign his or her agreement that states you agree to settle disputes by binding or nonbinding arbitration, I suggest you strike it out of the contract or run!

5. Never sign an agreement that makes you go out of your local area to seek justice. You may hear of this being called the venue. If they insist you must come to their place of venue or state to settle any disputes, I recommend you find another lawyer.

You also witnessed what happens in another state outside your own. Most folks and attorneys, too, will admit that judges are partial to individuals in their local state and if you are out of state, good luck.

Once again, if the attorney knows up front they might have to play their stink games in the presence of your local jury, I fully believe the attorney will act to an ethical standard more like what you should expect.

You saw what I recommended in the first chapter regarding an attorney's lack of a guarantee of any result . . . inserting the following in place of the lack of a guarantee cop-out clause:

> I solemnly swear or solemnly and sincerely affirm, as the case may be, that I will do nothing dishonest, and will not knowingly allow anything dishonest to be done in court, and that I will inform the court of any dishonesty of which I have knowledge; that I will not knowingly maintain or assist in maintaining any cause of action that is false or unlawful; that I will not obstruct any cause of action for personal gain or malice; but that I will exercise the office of attorney, in any court in which I may practice, according to the best of my learning and judgment, faithfully, to both my client and the court; so help me God or upon penalty of perjury, and I agree to abide by the Rules of Professional Conduct as provided by the American State Bar, and I will freely submit to civil or criminal prosecution in front of a public jury should my integrity ever become questioned.

So, within the judicial system of corruption, for goodness's sake, don't succumb to the weasel's way of granting the dodging of respectable legal performance standards upfront . . . because that's exactly what you are doing if you give them your signature.

The bottom line is, you better expect true professional representation for the price these jokers charge . . . otherwise you'll likely be far better off financially without an attorney who insists on having a cop-out "no guarantee of a result" clause in their retainer agreement. Don't do it!

6. For what little value that it's worth, check the State Bar for any disciplinary actions taken against an attorney you are considering using. If there is a record, the attorney must be really bad.

You have witnessed the actions of Mr. Quinn and see what his surrounding peers like the expert witness Mr. Pettit will testify to.

Again, I don't know how unearthly bad of a performance or unethical conduct an attorney would have to commit before even one of them on their jury panel of peers would admit they crossed the line and should require disciplinary action. Judge DiFiglia witnessed the whole mess and didn't act in the least, and did absolutely nothing other than ask the two attorneys how to get them all out of the mess he let them get into. You can expect absolutely no help from a judge.

The State Bar needs to go; it's a joke of its own!

7. Actually, I recommend you avoid signing a unilaterally generated retainer agreement with an attorney altogether.

Regardless of your matter, the importance of signing a unilaterally generated attorney agreement ought to scare the fire out of you regardless of whether you are experiencing a divorce or attempting a multibillion corporate lawsuit. This phenomenon of dealing with an attorney is one of the most important aspects of you giving up your rights and resultantly leaving your backside open to Mr. Ben Dover and Mr. C. Howlett Fields of the Dewey, Cheatem, and Howe Law Firms. I recommend you never sign an attorney retainer agreement without a complete and total review of all these change recommendations, and even then be fully capable of ditching the attorney without any strings attached to any future obligations, period!

After all, it was the great Thomas Jefferson who said, "It is the trade of lawyers to question everything, yield nothing, and to talk by the hour."

There needs to be some sense of uniformity of standards for the crimes and we as citizens must demand total reform to get back on the same page with equal rights for all—regardless of your pocket book depth!

Contact your representatives and senators and demand let's get back to some common sense basics, shall we? If you think it can't happen to you, just sit back on your laurels and wait until it happens to you and again, don't say something ignorant like, "I sure wish somebody would have told me about this."

8. Trust, trust, trust. (Don't trust.)

You can see what happens when you pride yourself as being a good and trusting client of an attorney and how you can be taken advantage of, so it ought to stand to reason that you should never give 100% trust into the hands of your hired and paid attorney because they likely are more interested in how much they can make off of you rather than what good they can do for you.

9. I would refrain from producing all your assets and total net value and giving it to your attorney at their request.

I don't care how uncomfortable this discussion becomes.

If your attorney wants to know how much you are worth, I'd tell them that information is private unless the attorney obtains a judge's order, and you would be held in contempt of court and fined for this. I would not give your attorney this information, period. Equal rights and justice should prevail for all according to our pledge of allegiance, if you truly believe it, regardless of your income and balance sheet.

10. If an attorney you are considering using does not have malpractice insurance, I recommend you keep looking for one who does.

You saw it and heard it from Mr. Coleman's own vantage point, and you know attorneys screw up quite frequently and think that is quite acceptable at any standard. Therefore, unless you never want to sue an attorney for profoundly ruining the chances for making your life financially whole, take kindly to notice whether or not he or she is covered with insurance to amend impacting your life accordingly as a result of any incompetent mistakes.

11. Send your attorney an IRS 1099 form for each year and every dollar and penny for their "professional" service, which is considered miscellaneous income, and report this to the IRS.

If you hire an attorney, spend an extra $20 to $30 and be responsible and be sure to do your own noble and patriotic duty and ensure your attorney pays his or her fair share of taxes. I might not have had the "power" to be able to prove that an attorney lied about anything in a court of law, but we Americans do have the power to ensure each and every attorney does their part to address the Federal deficit and to remind them they live in and do business in America and aren't above the law with respect to paying taxes. This is a matter of pleasure; at least it was for me!

12. Take heed to what happened in my case and use it for your own education, development of common sense knowledge, and the benefit of your own day-to-day dealings.

Try a little harder to resolve your issues on your own and exhaust as many other nonjudicial avenues as possible! I hope you never have to hire an attorney to resolve your differences with anyone. But if you do, you will have far lesser excuses for being victimized in the demented judicial profession.

13. Get some guts of your own and don't be afraid to be a whistle blower.

If everybody continues to play opossum, the chances of you getting the same royal treatment will remain large and there won't be much you'll be able to do about it either! If they want to continue lying, catch them and report it!

14. Ponder this. Demand new laws that would require both the suing client and the attorney to bear the total cost of the defense if they lose—win and you get your costs—in an effort to address tort reform.

I truly believe if this were the case, attorneys would stop their absurd shams on both sides and get to the factual evidence expeditiously. If Mr. Quinn knew he might have to pay 50% for all of the ABC defendants' fees including Mr. Kaeder's, I have my suspicions that those unanswered interrogatories after fourteen days might have been handled slightly different with Judge DiFiglia than just intentionally putting the order in the file for 11 months and surprising the judge at trial.

I totally believe this would also put a serious lid on today's perpetual litigation where only the attorneys currently win and victims lose regardless! So, don't bring an action unless you have just cause. And attorneys, don't do it unless you have your act together or you'll both lose. Fair enough?

• • •

I could only hope that our current Supreme Court justices go back to school and study up on what they missed . . . like the wisdom of Alexander Fraiser Tytler. Then, maybe our highest dignified Supreme Court justices might realize some very small, yet vitally important virtues that could save our ailing country.

I consider myself just getting started with my quest to expose the truth . . . for all. I welcome any and all support in addressing, to mention just a few, our judicial corruption, unequal rights, the lack of standards of tort and personal loss, self-serving attorneys on attorney discipline juries, lax penalty of perjury standards, the abolishment of the American Arbitration Association, the abolishment of the State Bar that is the biggest joke of the institution, the lifetime loss of the right to practice law for those who violate the codes of ethics which themselves need to be overhauled, and last but certainly not least—to restoring faith that there is a judicial watchdog in this country worthy of quality jokes slanted towards prosecution of the crooks instead of the victims, so we actually have law and order over farce and swindle.

Hopefully my eleven years of dedication and million-dollar loss will provide building blocks to repair the grossly fragmented judicial system. This country is full of hard-working and honest citizens who deserve some respect and appreciation, instead of being the brunt of pathetic attorney jokes. Open your eyes to the truth of corruption, the root of its origin, and take that first step of gathering the true facts. Then the rebuilding will begin.

ACKNOWLEDGMENTS

I would certainly like to recognize those attorneys and those people who made this book possible by their actions and their quoted excerpts which led me to write this book and expose our modern-day judicial system of juggernauts. Obviously without these individuals, this book never would have come to exist nor the factual information within. I owe my gratitude to each and every one of you for having some part of this historical event.

1. Darren J. Quinn: San Diego, CA/Del Mar, CA

    Thank you, Mr. Quinn, for you are the center of it all. You should be so proud of your actions that reflect upon your profession as a whole. Well done and documented, Mr. Quinn. Like Mr. Coleman at the end of the arbitration, I wish you well in your future practice as an attorney . . . because I think you are going to need a hell of a lot of help!

2. Paul M. DeCicco: San Diego, CA/Del Mar, CA

    Thank you, Mr. DeCicco, for all your rambling, which added to the humor of this book. I would especially like to thank you for your comment on your opinion of Mr. Quinn signing the last retainer agreement, stating that yes, Mr. Quinn received it, looked at it, signed it, and obviously stuffed it in a file, too. It was not binding Mr. Quinn to anything. I liked that; it really drives home one of my main points of my book here that I believe some of you attorneys really do consider yourselves able to alter or reinterpret contracts at whim—and consider yourselves above the law. Well done, Mr. DeCicco!

3. Douglas A. Pettit: San Diego, CA

Thank you, Mr. Pettit, for all your "expert witness" quotations. I'm confident the readers will all be impressed by your assessment of Mr. Quinn's performance. If Mr. Darren J. Quinn's performance was indeed excellent, I'd hate to see just how bad an attorney would have to be for you to truthfully testify to it.

4. Harold Coleman Jr., Esq.: San Diego, CA, and his case manager Lisa Allen-Cumiford of Fresno, CA

Thank you, Mr. Coleman, for your many quotations, clarifications, and rulings that were documented by the transcripts. Thank you for suggesting I move on and apply the "lessons learned" words of wisdom to my life. Your words inspired me and helped me decide to publish your actions so many can see your real true opinion of "not making the law," fair and balanced impartial ways of casting judgment of the law, and reflecting values of the people, especially when to it comes to your opinion of "fairness." Ever hear of the old saying, "what goes around, comes around"?

5. Kathrine Winn: San Diego, CA

Thank you, Ms. Winn, for your concerted effort, or should I say lack thereof, to ensure my three ring binder of evidence was not properly lodged with the court on appeal so it could never be used against Mr. Quinn. If there ever was an old cliché, "birds of a feather, stick together," I'd say you did a good job!

6. Gregory P. Goonan: San Diego, CA

Thank you, Mr. Goonan, for jumping on the band wagon of fleecing a fraud victim and jumping off when you are criticized for not applying any, and I mean any, of your supposedly high-level settlement skills to reduce the financial devastation in my situation.

7. Patrick F. O'Connor: La Mesa, CA

I do owe thanks with reservation to Mr. O'Connor. Mr. O'Connor did, in fact, act to set the wheels in motion for this matter. Mr. O'Connor reviewed the preliminary case information, what little I did have before I received my files from Quinn and before I paid to have the original trial transcripts made up.

8. George P. Andreos: San Diego, CA

Thank you, Mr. Andreos, for wanting $5,320 up front to file my first action against Mr. Quinn and failing to give me confidence you would file the case by the deadline I had to avoid the statute of limitations. Thanks for keeping $2,825 for accomplishing nothing. I appreciate the fact you withheld this $2,825 for providing absolutely no benefit to me. Thank you for adding to the list of attorneys who provided a background for this book.

9. John Rice: San Diego, CA

Thanks, Mr. Rice, for taking $500 to review my case information and not taking the case afterword. Mr. Rice actually provided the least amount of financial damage to me as any attorney in this case. Thanks for the minimal effect.

10. Thomas D. Mauriello: San Francisco, CA

    Mr. Mauriello recommended Mr. Darren J. Quinn to me.

11. Mike Brown: San Diego, CA

    I do want to thank Mr. Brown for truthfully testifying at the arbitration hearing about the fact no insurance policy ever existed. He is as honest as I have ever seen. We need more attorneys like him in the system to stand for truth—regardless of who violates the law! Thank you very much, Mr. Brown; you are a good man and an honest attorney! This man hasn't forgotten the "oath."

12. Bryan Sampson: San Diego, CA

    Thank you for your office telling me that Mr. Quinn screwed up on the appeal and you are the ones that told me the truth as to why Mr. Quinn lost the fabulous $2.7 million dollar claim damage. Thanks for determining that an insurance policy never existed as Mr. Quinn had represented.

13. Judge Jeffery B. Barton: San Diego, CA

    Thanks for denying me a chance to continue the arbitration matter with legal counsel and an expert. Thanks for denying the appeal Ms. Winn filed. For judges being known for not being able to give legal advice, I sure don't know how you can rule to the contrary! Thank you for your ruling in writing to support the arbitrator's decision.

14. Louis Oliver: Hendersonville, TN

    Thank you, Mr. Oliver, for first telling me you would help me even though you don't like to get involved in attorney billing dispute cases, then assisting both Mr. Goonan and Mr. Quinn to their benefit of "tort" as well as yourself . . . and not providing one penny of positive value to me over the period of nearly two years. Obviously, I believe you hold attorneys above the law. That is very clear to me.

15. Melody Black: Hendersonville, TN

Thank you, Ms. Black, for assisting me in drafting up a formal complaint to the California State Bar after I spoke with my local state representative, senator, and two attorney general senior attorneys. Thank you for the documentation trail leading to the result. The Supreme Court of the United States ruling is one readers will enjoy hopefully for years to come: "The petition is denied." Thank you for that important result, Melody!

16. Bruce Oldham, Gallatin, TN

You obviously couldn't have cared less as to what happened and how Mr. Quinn obtained his judgment against me. Thank you for applying the law of the land "RES JUDICATA" or also known as "Full Faith and Credit" of the Constitution of the United States— the matter had been previously decided in another state and can therefore not be argued any further on any grounds. Thank you for upholding the law of the land, Mr. Oldham. You are certainly no party whistle blower!

17. Dennis Dorman: San Diego, CA

Thank you, Mr. Dorman, for recognizing our judicial system is filled with schmucks. Mr. Dorman referred me to Ms. Winn who he thought was a straight shooter. You tried; I'll give you credit for that.

18. Kennen E. Kaeder: San Diego, CA

Oh, do I have a lot to thank Mr. Kaeder for. Mr. Kaeder provided one of the most colorful e-mail quotations for the benefit of the readers—the very conversation of the settlement discussion and what was really said but not consummated on the record.

19. Judge Vincent P. DiFiglia: San Diego, CA

Why didn't you at least demand a continuance of our trial until such time you and Mr. Quinn got it right? Yes, "it would have been nice." You overtly failed to demand justice! Mr. DiFiglia, you were a judge, you knew or should have well known there are ethical conduct rules pertaining to such ridiculous court procedures.

20. Ben Perry: Nashville, TN

Let's not forget about the fresh and new addition to the herd, Mr. Perry, who did what Mr. Lewis Oliver wouldn't—sue Mr. Quinn for breaking the law! Mr. Perry is my hero. See, there are good attorneys out there who deserve a better reputation!

I would also like to recognize those individuals who assisted in the search for justice and were an integral part of laying the historical tracks that have been assimilated in this book.

Former Tennessee State Representative, Susan Lynn: Thank you, Ms. Lynn, for highly recommending that I write this book and for claiming it should indeed become a "best seller." America needs judicial reform—now!

Former Tennessee Senator, Diane Black

Two Tennessee State Attorney Generals' office female attorneys—names unknown: Although these two could not get involved because this issue was an out-of-state issue, they recommended using an attorney to draft and file another complaint with the California State Bar, which I did.

Jesse Cisneros of the California State Bar, who assisted with my return of file complaint and the instructional directive to Mr. Quinn to give me my files.

John Meno, Collection attorney working with Mr. Sampson: San Diego, CA: Thank you, Mr. Meno, for providing me with the truth, the appellate court ruling, which revealed Mr. Quinn losing the $2.7 million dollar claim and why. Otherwise, I may not have ever found out.

I can say, many other attorneys would not take the case solely because Mr. Quinn did not have malpractice insurance—and for that reason alone. Interesting or dishonorable? You be the judge.

It might be possible to locate some of these attorneys by searching for attorneys at the following law firm:

Ben Dover and
C. Howlett Fields
Attorneys at Law

GOOD EATING

A man walked into a bar with his alligator and asked the bartender, "Do you serve lawyers here?"

"Sure do," replied the bartender.

"Good," said the man. "Give me a beer, and I'll have a lawyer for my gator."